AIRCRAFT INDUSTRY DYNAMICS

An Analysis of Competition, Capital, and Labor

BARRY BLUESTONE
PETER JORDAN
MARK SULLIVAN

Social Welfare Research Institute
Boston College

Auburn House Publishing Company
Boston, Massachusetts

Prepared under the auspices of the Joint Center for Urban Studies of MIT and Harvard University, this book is based on a report prepared for the Office of Economic Analysis and Research, Economic Development Administration, U.S. Department of Commerce, under grant number OER-620-G78-14 (99-7-13440). The work was co-sponsored by the Office of Research and Development, Employment and Training Administration, U.S. Department of Labor; and the Center for the Study of Metropolitan Problems, National Institutes of Mental Health, U.S. Department of Health, Education, and Welfare. The statements, findings, conclusions, and recommendations do not necessarily reflect the views of any of the sponsoring agencies.

Library of Congress Cataloging in Publication Data
Bluestone, Barry.
  Aircraft industry dynamics.

  Bibliography: p.
  Includes index.
  1. Aircraft industry—United States.
I. Jordan, Peter, 1956-   II. Sullivan, Mark.
III. Title.
HD9711.U6B58   338.4'7629133'0973   81-2118
ISBN 0-86569-053-7   AACR2

Printed in the United States of America

PREFACE

This book is based on a case study of the U.S. aircraft industry completed under a broad program of research on economic development. The program was sponsored by the Economic Development Administration of the U.S. Department of Commerce, the Employment and Training Administration of the U.S. Department of Labor, and the Center for the study of Metropolitan Problems (now the Center for Work and Mental Health), a division of the National Institutes of Mental Health of the U.S. Department of Health and Human Services. The original research was undertaken at the MIT–Harvard University Joint Center for Urban Studies in cooperation with MIT's Department of Urban Studies and Planning and its Sloan School of Management, and with the Social Welfare Research Institute at Boston College. The long list of sponsors and the number of universities involved in the project provide some idea of the magnitude of the research effort initially undertaken.

The original project was built upon the premise that one can understand the dynamics of an economy only by understanding the nature of its industries. The research staff, under the direction of Professor Bennett Harrison of MIT, opted for an analytic strategy based on individual industry case studies. The industries chosen for investigation were carefully selected on the basis of each industry's contribution to regional economic growth. The aircraft industry was selected because of its central importance as a manufacturing employer, its economic volatility, and because of its leadership role in the high technology sector.

In a period in which we see the bedrock industries of America—automobile, steel, and rubber—undergoing the worst turmoil in recent economic history, the aircraft industry stands out as a clear example of American dominance in world markets. The modern jet aircraft is as much a global symbol of America as are the Stars and Stripes. A Boeing 727 sitting on a runway in Abu Dhabi or Caracas is as familiar as one in Albuquerque or Chicago.

Indeed, as a world exporter the aircraft industry has no peer in the U.S. manufacturing sector. It now contributes over $10 billion annually to the U.S. balance of payments, while it employs more than a million workers in the design, construction, and testing of aircraft, aircraft engines, and parts. Only the automobile industry employs a larger number of manufacturing workers in the United States.

Yet naturally, even this flourishing sector of the U.S. economy is not without a host of problems, some akin to those confronting other mature industries and some quite different. Because of the on-again, off-again nature of military procurement and the "re-equipment" cycle characteristic of the commercial market, the industry has always been prone to extreme sales and employment volatility. For example, aircraft sales nearly doubled between 1964 and 1968, before plummeting by nearly a third during the following three years. Internally the industry faces massive layoffs during its periodic slumps; during the ensuing recoveries, it increasingly faces shortages of exotic raw materials and skilled labor. Although it has experienced these types of problems since at least the first World War, neither its leaders nor those in government have uncovered the secret to smoothing out the cycle or adequately dealing with its consequences.

The industry is unique in terms of its organizational structure. While there are extremely few competitors in the airframe or aircraft engine markets, giving the industry near-monopoly status, the rivalry between the few firms in the market is more intense than in most other sectors of the economy. The winning or losing of a single major contract can often spell success or failure for the firm. As a result, interfirm rivalry has all the intrigue of a good spy novel, with billions of dollars in sales, millions in profit, and thousands of jobs at stake in every competition.

Still, with all of its peculiarities, this industry has many lessons for the American economy, especially in a period of economic re-evaluation and "reindustrialization." As a leader in the high technology sector and as a successful international competitor, it has an engaging tale to tell about life in the new international economic order. One can expect that more and more analysts will be turning to this sector to gain some insight into the possibilities and the perils that face American industry in the coming decade. We hope that this book will provide some valuable information not only to those who have an interest in this fascinating industry but also to those who are concerned with economic development and the health of the American economy.

BARRY BLUESTONE
March 15, 1981   BOSTON COLLEGE

ACKNOWLEDGMENTS

Every step in the development of this book benefited from the nurturance of our colleagues at MIT, Harvard, and Boston College. New England Economy Project staff meetings held at the Joint Center for Urban Studies helped us formulate questions and untangle mysteries as they arose in our research. While all of the staff gave us help at one time or another, special thanks are due Professor Bennett Harrison, the project's Principal Investigator. Ben gave us constant encouragement and, on many occasions, coaxed us to probe deeper into complex issues.

Our promise of strict anonymity to our industry sources prevents us from listing the names of the dozens of company officials, industry experts, and union officials who gave of their time and insight so that we might bolster this research with fresh information and accurately reflect the current status of the industry. Our personal thanks are offered to all of you.

As for our own staff at the Social Welfare Research Institute, we want to express once again our gratitude. Special thanks are due Alan Matthews, Ann Grenell, Tom Barbera, Mark Cullinane, Amy Kruser, Tim Benell, Katherine Shea, and Mary Ellen Schriver. Finally, the three of us wish to express our deepest appreciation to Virginia Richardson, who supervised the overall production of the monograph that became the basis of this book.

BARRY BLUESTONE

CONTENTS

ix

LIST OF FIGURES

LIST OF TABLES

Chapter 1

INTRODUCTION

The day after the landslide presidential victory of Ronald Reagan the New York Stock Exchange soared to its highest sales volume in history. More than 84 million shares were traded before the day was over. Defense issues led all stocks that gained in value as analysts expected the new Reagan administration to pursue a stronger defense posture. Boeing Aircraft, which opened late in the session, was the second most active issue with a volume of more than one million shares. Boeing's price climbed by 1⅛ before trading on the Big Board closed. Among other defense issues, United Technologies spurted 3⅞ points, Rockwell International 3½, and LTV ½, all in active trading. No defense stocks fared poorly. Big gainers included McDonnell Douglas, up 2 full points, Northrup, up 4⅜, and Martin Marietta, up 3¾. Not far behind were other prime defense contractors, including General Electric, one of the two major producers of aircraft engines; Thiokol, Avco Corp., and TRW, likely prime contractors for the MX missile system; and Fairchild Industries, Grumman, and Textron, manufacturers of military jet aircraft and helicopters.

For many defense workers, the Reagan victory was comforting. This was particularly true for aircraft workers, whose jobs historically have been among the most insecure of all manufacturing jobs in the United States. Presidential elections, congressional politics, and international affairs can send the industry soaring or put it into a tailspin. Literally hundreds of thousands of jobs can disappear in a matter of months. Multibillion-dollar corporations can go from high-flyers on the stock exchange to bankruptcy as a result of betting on the wrong aircraft design or merely by being six months behind the competition with a new generation of equipment.

1

This volatility is by no means limited to the military sphere. Commercial production also has its cycle, a product of global economic conditions and airline re-equipment requirements. In 1970 and 1971 Boeing—by far the leading commercial jet manufacturer—nearly collapsed after four years of sales growth spurred by production of its 747 jumbo jet and its smaller 727. Employment plunged from nearly 100,000 to 37,000, devastating not only the company, but also much of Seattle, Washington, its home base. It was not until late in the decade that Boeing began to experience a full economic recovery. On the strength of orders that began arriving in 1978 and 1979 for its new long-range 767 aircraft, Boeing's employment and profits began to expand again. Its fortunes improved still further when in November 1980 it won the largest single commercial order in history, a $3 billion sale to Delta Airlines for 60 of its mid-range 757 jets. Only four weeks later, American Airlines contributed to Boeing's full-scale boom with an order for 45 more of these aircraft.[1] The sale also meant a resurgence of Pratt & Whitney's commercial jet engine division, which had been under serious market pressure from General Electric. Delta and American both opted for P&W's PW2037 engine as the power plant for their 757s, giving the United Technologies division over a billion dollars in sales.[2]

This economic roller coaster is nothing new for the U.S. aircraft industry. In 1939, two years before Pearl Harbor, the entire aircraft industry employed only 63,000 workers. More workers were involved in the production of tires and inner tubes and four times as many were producing shoes. Aircraft and Parts [Standard Industrial Classification (SIC) 372] provided jobs for only one out of every 167 workers in manufacturing.[3] Four years later, at the height of the war, there were 21 times as many workers in the industry. The feverishly paced production of B-17 Flying Fortresses, B-24 Liberators, P-51 Mustangs, P-38 Lightnings, and P-47 Thunderbolts made aircraft the single largest industry in the nation. Nearly one out of every 13 workers in the manufacturing labor force was employed in this sector.

At the end of the war, the industry collapsed. Employment plummeted from a peak of 1.46 million in November 1943 to 219,000 in March 1946. The 23 aircraft engine firms that had sprung up to service the airframe producers during the war dwindled to five by December of the following year.[4] Having already gone through this boom-and-bust pattern during World War I, the spectacular decline was neither unusual nor unforeseen. For this reason, it was expected that after Viet-Nam there would be a similar downturn in the aircraft market, and indeed there was. During the war, the value of aircraft shipments in real terms rose from $13.4 billion in 1960 to a high of $22.1 billion in 1968 before falling virtually in half by 1975. Employment rode the same roller coaster, rising from 678,000 to 810,000 and then collapsing to levels much lower than those prevailing before the nation's full-scale military involvement.[5] Figure 1.1 displays graphically the intense volatility in this industry. By 1968 employment was nearly 40 percent higher than in 1965; in 1977 total employment was only 75 percent of the index year.

Other industries may be as volatile, but surely none is as large and politically important as the aircraft industry. In a nation that has had such a romance with the automobile, it is seldom realized that aircraft is the second largest employer in U.S. manufacturing. With over 650,000 workers in 1980, it was the second leading (3-digit) employer following the auto industry, and certainly the largest among employers of skilled blue-collar machinists, engineers, and technicians. Added to as many as 400,000 aircraft workers in related industries categorized in other standard industrial classifications, there are at least a million workers involved in the design and production of airframes, engines, and parts.

The Nature of the Industry

The aircraft industry is part of the so-called high technology sector. It is an industry in which the sophistication of the product is being continually enhanced. Actual production is accomplished on a unit-by-unit basis rather than on an assembly line or as part of a continuous process operation. The materials and machinery used in production are often exotic, the tolerances precise, and the performance criteria stringent. Firms within the industry manufacture thousands of individual products, ranging from enormous airframes and immense jet turbines to a myriad array of parts and fixtures.

To gain a better sense of the industry, it is helpful to understand

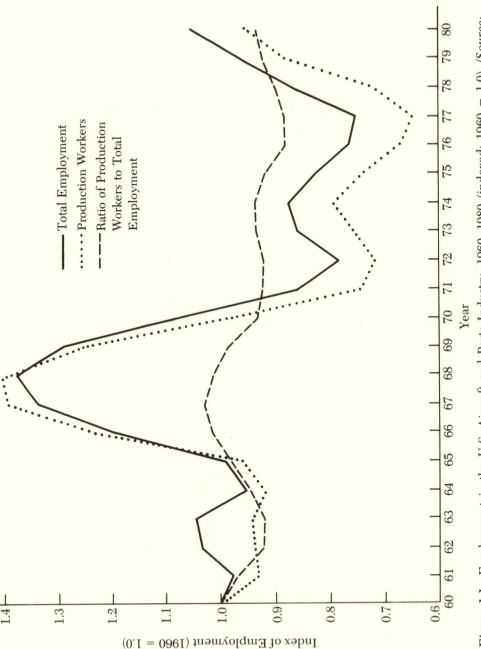

Figure 1.1 Employment in the U.S. Aircraft and Parts Industry, 1960–1980 (indexed: 1960 = 1.0). (*Source:* Employment and Earnings in the United States, *Bureau of Labor Statistics, U.S. Department of Labor.*)

its individual divisions. Aircraft and Parts (SIC 372) is composed of the following three sectors.*

> SIC 3721—*Aircraft*—*Establishments primarily engaged in manu-facturing or assembling complete aircraft. This sector also includes establishments primarily engaged in re-search and development on aircraft or in factory-type aircraft modification on a contract or fee basis.*
>
> SIC 3724—*Aircraft Engines and Engine Parts*—*Establishments primarily engaged in manufacturing aircraft engines and parts. Research and development on aircraft en-gines is included in this sector.*
>
> SIC 3728—*Aircraft Parts and Auxiliary Equipment, not elsewhere classified*—*Establishments primarily engaged in man-ufacturing aircraft parts and auxiliary equipment not elsewhere classified. Research and development on air-craft parts is included in this sector.†*

Although the entire industry is the second largest manufacturing employer in the country, production is so geographically concen-trated that its primary impact is felt only in certain regions. In 1972 over 94 percent of the value of complete commercial aircraft shipments came from the West Coast, notably the states of Wash-ington and California.[6] It is here that Boeing, McDonnell Douglas, and Lockheed are located, the big three (and indeed the only three) large commercial airframe producers in the United States. The manufacture of military aircraft is more geographically dis-persed, with the South producing 41 percent of all shipments, the West 22 percent, and the rest of the country the remainder.

Aircraft engine production, a totally separate division of the industry, is overwhelmingly located in New England and the Mid-West. These two regions (and in particular the areas around Lynn, Massachusetts, and Evendale, Ohio, where General Electric has facilities, and central Connecticut, the home of Pratt & Whitney) manufacture over 95 percent of the jet turbines purchased by the U.S. military and a majority of all other aircraft propulsion

---

* See the appendix for a complete listing of the products of each of these three sectors.

† Besides Aircraft and Parts (SIC 372) there is also SIC 376, Guided Missiles and Space Vehicles. Together the two 3-digit SIC categories are often referred to as the "aerospace" industry. In this study, neither guided missiles nor space vehicles will receive any detailed analysis; however, limited reference will be made to them throughout the text as necessity dictates. The reader should note that when the term aerospace is used, it refers to SIC 372 and SIC 376 combined.

units. New England—notably Connecticut and Massachusetts—was responsible for almost 45 percent of all engine parts and accessories, whereas the Northeast (including New York, New Jersey, and Pennsylvania) was responsible for one third of all research and development of aircraft parts. As a result, the aircraft industry is located primarily on the Atlantic and Pacific coasts, airframes being produced in the West while their power plants are manufactured in the traditional capital-intensive areas of the Northeast and Mid-West. The two major exceptions to this lopsided distribution are private business aircraft production in the Midwest and military aircraft production in the South. This geographical pattern was first established in the early days of piston engine biplanes and is maintained today in an era of supersonic turbojets.

The Current State of the Aircraft Industry

After being depressed for the better part of the 1970s, the aircraft industry today is experiencing another periodic boom. Department of Defense procurement of military aircraft, which was under $7 billion in 1978, is expected to exceed $12 billion in fiscal 1981.[7] This growth comes in the wake of an increase in total aircraft and parts sales from $15.9 billion in 1976 to more than $24 billion in 1979. Backlogged orders present an even more impressive picture. By 1979 total orders for aircraft, engines, and parts exceeded $48 billion, a figure recorded before the announcement of large sales to Delta and American Airlines in late 1980.[8]

As a result of this healthy sales boom, the industry's net profit after taxes, measured as a percentage of sales, reached 5.1 percent in 1979, up from 4.4 percent in the previous year. This profit rate was only slightly below that of all U.S. manufacturing.[9] Indeed, net profits as a percentage of sales and as a percentage of stockholders's equity were higher than at any time in the past 20 years.[10] At 19.1 percent, the net profits to equity ratio actually exceeded that for all manufacturing. Part of the discrepancy between the two profit figures can be explained by the fact that a portion of the capital used in the aerospace industry is provided at government expense rather than from private sources.

In 1979 the aerospace industry also set new records for export sales and net trade balance. With a trade surplus of $10.1 billion, aerospace led all U.S. manufacturing industries in its positive contribution to the nation's trade balance.[11] Only the agricultural sector contributed more to offsetting the domestic trade deficit. Exports of aerospace products outstripped imports by a factor of seven to one. With total exports at $11.7 billion, civilian exports constituted 83 percent of the total. Of this amount, $6.2 billion was for aircraft, $3.2 billion for parts, accessories, and equipment, and $375 million for engines.[12]

Not surprisingly, Boeing Aircraft was the leading exporter of all companies in the United States. Nearly half of Boeing's total 1979 sales ($8.1 billion) were made to foreigners.[13] Boeing was not alone, however. Five of the leading 10 export firms in the nation were aircraft or aircraft engine producers (Boeing, General Electric, McDonnell Douglas, United Technologies, and Lockheed). With the Boeing 757 and 767, this position can only improve.

Still the question remains as to how long the present boom will last. Here, again, there are too many imponderables to give a precise estimate. The length of the boom depends on whether defense spending continues to escalate, how much oil price increases encourage airlines to re-equip with fuel-efficient planes, whether interest rates remain high, and whether there is continued economic stagnation, which leads to flat or declining airline revenues. Nevertheless, the sheer size of the backlogged order book suggests that the boom can last at least into the mid to late 1980s, with the commercial sphere leading the way.

The Dynamics of the Industry

The aircraft industry, seen as a particular form of industrial organization, is truly unique in the American economy. No other industry of comparable size is composed of firms perched so precariously between fortune and failure, and with the notable exception of the auto industry, no other industry is forced by technological necessity to make billion-dollar investments so fraught with risk. First appearances suggest that the domestic aircraft industry is a classic oligopoly with only three commercial airframe manufacturers and two large thrust jet engine producers. Indeed, the industry often appears to be the closest thing we have to a monopoly, rivaling the industrial structure of the utility sector.

Compared to General Motors, which is responsible for 20 percent of the world auto market, and IBM, which has 30 percent of the world computer dollar, Boeing is clearly more dominant in its own market. For many years Boeing has sold 50 to 55 percent of all commercial airliners, and now with its 757 and 767 it may likely increase its share to 65 to 70 percent.[14] Pratt & Whitney boasted a similar dominant position in the jet engine market for an even longer period of time.

Yet despite this quasi-monopoly position, the aircraft industry marketplace is known for its fierce rivalry. The competitive dynamics of the industry are such that seldom does more than one manufacturer dominate the market for commercial airliners or power plants during a specific generation. In the 1930s and 1940s the Douglas DC-3 virtually monopolized world commercial air travel. In the late 1950s Boeing assumed the dominant role in this market. In the jet engine market, it was Pratt & Whitney's famous "Wasp" engine that powered an overwhelming proportion of World War II aircraft. The same company powered the first and second generation of commercial jet aircraft before General Electric began to challenge it in the mid-1970s. Dominance by a single firm in the military sector is less pronounced only because the federal government has taken precautions to maintain multiple sources for its defense goods.

The enormous capital requirements, and increasingly the crucial race to get into the market first with a new product, explain both the oligopolistic nature of the industry and the intense rivalry between the limited number of firms. To maintain its dominance in the commercial power plant business, for example, Pratt & Whitney is spending over $1 billion to develop its JT10D turbine, newly renamed the PW2037. Boeing, McDonnell Douglas, and Lockheed routinely spend at least this amount to develop new airframes and bring them from conception through model design to production. Moreover, although the birth of a new product often requires an investment of this magnitude and a gestation period sometimes lasting a decade or more, a six-month delay in introducing a new generation of equipment can cost a manufacturer 60 percent or more of the total market. Thus timing is of the utmost importance. The Douglas DC-8 followed Boeing's 707 into commercial use by less than a year, but the delay was sufficient to provide Boeing with the lion's share of the original commercial jet market, which it has maintained ever since. The story of Lockheed's L-1011 is similar; although many industry experts suggest that this aircraft is superior to the McDonnell Douglas DC-10, its late introduction doomed unit sales to well below the break-even point. By 1979 there were only 160 L-1011s in service worldwide compared to 276 DC-10s.[15] Given the costs of development, the break-even point for these aircraft is said to be in the vicinity of 300 planes.

Marketing in the Aircraft Industry

Selling in the aircraft industry is done very differently from that in other product markets. Price turns out to play a reasonably minor role in both commercial and military aircraft sales, whereas performance, maintainability, and, most importantly, on-time delivery will often decide who reigns as the current king of the mountain or who drops out of the market completely.

With the possible exception of the ordnance industry, no other industry is more dependent on government policy and government purchasing power for its livelihood than aircraft. The sheer volume of government hardware procurement and research and development funding has produced an industry that is largely a monopsony—an industry that has only one primary customer. Indeed, in 8 of the 14 years between 1966 and 1979, the U.S. government purchased the majority of all aircraft and engines produced.[16] For individual companies, the value of defense contracts is staggering. The net value of government contracts to General Dynamics, for example, exceeded $3.5 billion in 1979 alone. McDonnell Douglas earned over $3.2 billion from the government for F-4, F-15, and F-18 fighter aircraft. United Technologies, General Electric, Lockheed, Hughes Aircraft, Boeing, and Grumman all enjoyed $1.4 billion or more in government support.[17]

Because of this factor, the level of industry shipments, investment, and employment are in large part politically determined. Domestic military aircraft sales are directly subject to congressional debate over the size and distribution of the defense budget. In addition, foreign military orders, a growing share of all shipments, are controlled by State Department politics and the stability of allies and "friendly" governments. The level of aircraft sales in the near future is likely to depend on the final resolution of a SALT treaty.

Even in the commercial sphere, government influence plays an important role. The new generation of passenger and cargo transports represented by the Boeing 757 and 767 and the European Airbus series is obviously a response to skyrocketing fuel costs and fuel shortages, but federal and local government regulations on noise and engine effluents were no less important in promulgating the current boom in sales. Likewise, the sale of commercial jets to foreign airlines is tied inextricably to political decisions. Non-tariff barriers to trade have become critical in determining which firm's jet engines go into which airframes. Relative to all of these political factors, fluctuations in GNP, business taxation, and materials, energy, and labor costs play only an indirect role in determining short-run aggregate levels of investment, aircraft shipments, and employment.

The Location of Production

The overall level of production and investment is one matter; its location is potentially quite another, affecting the growth and decline of individual regions of the country. Enormous fixed costs sunk in the plant and equipment of prime contractors generally preclude any large-scale capital flight similar to that which occurred in the textile, clothing, and footwear industries. There are also some lingering "agglomeration economies" that maintain Massachusetts, Connecticut, Southern California, and Washington as key locations for prime and subcontractors.

Nevertheless, the web of aircraft production is spreading out around the country and in fact the world, most notably to Europe and Japan. Data for New England aircraft industry shipments and value added provide one vivid example of the relocation of production. Between 1965 and 1976, New England's share of total U.S. aircraft shipments grew by nearly 26 percent. In contrast, the amount of value added actually produced in the region grew by only 8.4 percent.[18] This disparity reflects the fact that the ratio of value added to value of shipments in New England plunged from nearly 58 percent in 1965 to barely 46 percent in 1976. Consequently, less of the final value of shipments is actually being manufactured in New England, while a growing proportion is

Table 1.1   New England Aircraft Industry—Vital Statistics

	1965	*1976*	% Δ
Value of Shipments (Real)	$1.55b	$1.55b	0%
Value Added (Real)	$892 m	$713 m	− 20.1
All Employees	65,600	54,900	− 16.6
Production Workers	41,500	34,300	− 17.3

SOURCE: *Annual Survey of Manufacturers*, 1965, 1976.

being made elsewhere and shipped to the region for final assembly. The implications for employment are obvious. With the value of shipments in real terms essentially unchanged between 1965 and 1976, real value added in New England fell by 20 percent and total employment declined by a sixth (see Table 1.1).

Three reasons for the decline in New England's share of actual production should be noted. One is a secular reduction in the make/buy ratio among the primes. This ratio indicates the degree to which prime contractors buy, rather than produce in-house, parts that will go into their final product. At one time, manufacturers were responsible for producing 60 percent or more of the value of a complete airframe or aircraft engine. Today, most prime contractors admit to being much less self-contained, buying 50 percent or more of the parts that go into the final product.

A second and related reason involves the geographical dispersion of subcontractors. In an earlier period, a larger proportion of parts manufacturers were found in the immediate vicinity of the primes. With tremendous reductions in long-distance transportation and communication costs, it has become feasible to import parts cost-effectively from other regions of the country and from all over the world. Of the nearly 600 major parts subcontractors used by one of New England's large jet turbine producers, more than 63 percent are now located outside the region, and at least 18 of these firms are foreign vendors.

The third reason for dispersion of the aircraft industry involves the penetration of international politics and finance into the market. Despite the massive balance of trade surplus generated by the industry, knowledgeable sources admit that there is no such thing as an "American aircraft engine" any longer, and it is doubtful that one can call even a Boeing jet a uniquely American product. A whole new vocabulary is needed to describe this phenomenon: joint ventures, licensing arrangements, co-production, and offset agreements.

Multinational joint ventures are pursued by airframe and jet turbine manufacturers as a way of sharing development costs and spreading individual risk. In order to develop a new jet engine, for example, a firm (or division) may spend its total net worth or more for design and tooling. According to industry sources, this "bet your company" vulnerability has made it too expensive for a single firm to undertake such investment. Anti-trust laws prohibit certain types of joint ventures among U.S. prime contractors, thus providing domestic producers with an incentive to seek out foreign partners.

International licensing arrangements are also being embraced as foreign countries develop their own sophisticated tooling capacity. Under the terms of a recent sale of 100 F-15 fighters to the Japanese Self-Defense Force, Pratt & Whitney agreed to grant Ishikawajima-Harima a license to manufacture 205 F-100-PW-100 engines (including spares) for 78 of the 100 planes.[19] This licensing agreement allows Pratt & Whitney to reap a satisfactory return on its R&D investment in the F100 engine without expanding its production facilities or hiring additional labor for this special run.

Co-production, however, is the fastest growing institution in the international aircraft market. Foreign governments are demanding that a share of production take place within their own borders. With most foreign air carriers government-owned, balance of payment effects and job creation are major considerations in awarding contracts for both commercial and military aircraft. Some recent foreign contracts carry a co-production responsibility as high as 58 percent.[20] Aircraft company representatives, as well as trade union officials, have asserted that if it were not for these particular non-tariff trade restrictions, much more production would be carried on domestically. One jet engine manufacturer has indicated that the expense of producing one of their engines in Europe runs nearly 130 percent of the U.S. cost because of more expensive European labor and the need for redundant capital facilities. Presumably the additional cost is added into the contract price so the chief victim is the domestic aircraft workforce, not corporate profits. Over the long term, however, even profits may suffer as the result of increased foreign competition made possible by the transfer of U.S. technology to international co-production and licensing partners.

New Production Strategies and Their Consequences

To comply with the market imperatives of first to market, on-time delivery, and international competition, aircraft manufacturers are resorting to new strategies. Almost all are attempting to assure on-time contract compliance by seeking to eliminate sources of potential disruption of production, particularly with respect to their own labor force and their subcontractors. "Multiple sourcing" (that is, contracting with several suppliers for identical parts) has flourished, often despite a sacrifice of scale economies. Similarly, "parallel production" facilities within the same company have been established, especially if one unit is already operating under union contract. Both multiple sourcing and parallel production represent attempts to minimize potential disruption by providing back-up capacity in the event of subcontractor failure or work stoppage. This phenomenon naturally manifests itself in the dispersion of manufacturing and very likely explains why employment in older locations like New England has declined.

The first victims of relocation are the local subcontractors who have traditionally been the "tail on the industry dog" and who have borne the brunt of the aircraft sector's volatility. The prime contractors have always varied their make/buy ratios counter-cyclically in order to stabilize their own employment at the expense of their vendors. This new competitive strategy suggests that even now, during the growth phase of the cycle, existing suppliers will be forced to share subcontracts with a more geographically dispersed constellation of parts makers. Labor, of course, is affected as well, as is clearly observable in the current expansion.

Aircraft Industry Dynamics and the Labor Force

The nature of competition in the aircraft industry, the high degree of sales volatility, the dispersion of the subcontractor network, the growth of parallel production facilities, and the spread of co-production, joint venture, and licensing agreements have all had a significant impact on the industry's labor force. During contractions, such as occurred between 1968 and 1972 when total employment plummeted by over 370,000 workers or 45 percent, whole regions of the country are plunged into depression. Until expansion begins again, both families and communities must limp along on depressed incomes and tight local government budgets. Companies also suffer, trying to find ways to keep their most skilled workers employed so as not to lose them permanently.

When the cycle begins to reverse, workers and their communities immediately benefit, but new problems face the firm. To fulfill orders, companies must be able to locate and hire skilled workers ranging from engineers and designers to blue-collar machinists. Until the 1970s this posed little problem because of the surplus of skilled workers trained during World War II. But since the post–Viet-Nam recession, companies have found it increasingly difficult to hire needed workers. The universal complaint both on the West Coast and in New England has been an alleged inadequate supply of skilled engineers and skilled production workers. The World War II "vintage" worker is now retired and there is an apparent inadequate resupply, especially among skilled machinists and machine operators. The use of computerized machinery, the dispersion of production to new regions, and the expansion of international production have not as yet filled the gap between labor demand and labor supply. The training of a new generation of workers is apparently well behind schedule, the result of inadequate planning, a lack of government aid in this area, and the inherent problems of individual firms paying privately for the general training of workers.

For less-skilled production employees, the dynamics of the industry pose other problems. New technology and the dispersal of production threaten to displace an ever-growing number of workers from their jobs. The ratio of production workers to nonproduction workers has continued to decline since the mid-1960s as aircraft and engines become more technically sophisticated and production techniques become less labor intensive. As a consequence, the industry, both in good times and in bad, is providing fewer and fewer well-paying production jobs to workers of average skill. Along with similar trends in autos, steel, rubber, and the rest of the core manufacturing sector, this poses long-run problems for a substantial number of workers in the economy. In this sense, the aircraft industry once again provides an excellent case study in what the future may hold for the American economy.

Summary

All of this is by way of introduction to the U.S. aircraft industry, the second largest manufacturing industry in the nation. It is meant to raise a number of issues concerning cyclical volatility, political determination of aggregate output levels, the relationship between prime contractors and subcontractors, the proliferation of multiple sourcing and parallel production, and the growing internationalization of the industry. The real questions, of course, are still to be examined. What does all this mean for the future of the industry, for the leading firms in it, and for the workers and communities whose fate is tied to the vagaries of the aircraft market? Exploration of these questions is the subject matter for the balance of this volume.

In Chapter 2 we present a brief history of the aircraft industry from its origins before World War I to the full-fledged modern structure that evolved after World War II. Chapter 3 is devoted to a more complete discussion of the industry's transformation in the post–World War II era. The nature of competition and the industrial dynamics of the industry are explored in Chapter 4. This chapter sets the stage for understanding capital investment, the spatial location of production, and the specialized technology used in the industry, all of which are discussed in Chapter 5. To complete our investigation of aircraft industry dynamics, Chapter 6 is devoted to the issue of employment and labor force trends in the industry, with special emphasis on the New England jet engine sector. The importance of government relations is explored in Chapter 7. All of this material is finally reviewed in Chapter 8, in which we also present forecasts about the future directions of the industry.

The lessons that can be learned from understanding the aircraft industry go far beyond airframes and jet engines. As we hope to show, deciphering the dynamics of this industry can provide insights into the future of the entire American economic system.

Endnotes

1. William M. Carley, "Boeing Reign in Skies May Last a Long Time as Competition Fades," *Wall Street Journal*, December 19, 1980, p. 1.
2. "Pratt & Whitney Gets $450m. Pact from American," *Boston Globe*, December 23, 1980, p. 36.

3. *Employment and Earnings Statistics for the United States 1909–1968*, Bureau of Labor Statistics, U.S. Department of Labor, Bulletin No. 1312–6, August 1968.

4. John B. Rae, *Climb to Greatness: The American Aircraft Industry, 1920–1960* (Cambridge, Mass.: MIT Press, 1968), p. 173.

5. *Annual Survey of Manufacturers*, U.S. Bureau of the Census, 1960–1976.

6. These and the following regional statistics were calculated from U.S. Bureau of the Census, *Census of Manufacturers*, 1972.

7. Aerospace Industries Association, *Aerospace Facts and Figures 1980/81*, p. 26.

8. *Ibid.*, p. 15.

9. *Ibid.*, p. 9.

10. IAM Research Department, "1980 IAM Aerospace Report Economic Outlook," International Association of Machinists, April 1980, p. 5.

11. *Aerospace Facts and Figures*, p. 11.

12. *Ibid.*

13. Nancy Welles, "The 50 Leading Exporters," *Fortune Magazine*, September 22, 1980, p. 115.

14. *Wall Street Journal*, December 19, 1980, p. 1.

15. *Aerospace Facts and Figures*, p. 76.

16. *Ibid.*, p. 15.

17. Richard Halloran, "Why Defense Costs So Much," *New York Times*, January 11, 1981, p. F1.

18. Calculated from the U.S. Bureau of the Census, *Annual Survey of Manufacturers*, 1965–1976.

19. *Aviation Week and Space Technology*, April 23, 1979.

20. David Boulton, *F16: Sale of the Century* (Boston, Mass.: WGBH Education Foundation, 1979), p. 8.

Chapter 2

A HISTORY OF THE AIRCRAFT INDUSTRY TO 1950

Before World War I the original aeronauts—the Orville and Wilbur Wrights, the Glenn Curtisses, and the Igor Sikorskys—were busy handcrafting their own unique flying machines. While the Kaiser organized the Prussian states, the ranks of these pioneers multiplied. "Aeronautical companies" were soon to be found throughout the industrial world, although the assembly of individual airplanes hardly constituted an industry. In the early days, anybody with the daring, engineering expertise, and minimal resources could build these contraptions in their garages. Operations were housed in barns, stables, or anywhere an inventor found space. The initial gains came in the form of self-satisfaction and technological advance, rather than financial profit.

The First Era of Growth

This era of conception lasted no longer than a decade. In 1914 the exigencies of warfare engendered the first genuine market opportunity. As orders came in from European nations embroiled in World War I sooner than the United States, the federal government paved the way for a quantum growth in production. The National Advisory Committee for Aeronautics (NACA) was formed to serve as liaison between the industry and government. Recognizing the strategic importance of aircraft, it established NACA to rationalize the haphazard structure of the industry and put production on a profit-making basis. The creation of this agency symbolized the first of many attempts by the government to shelter

17

the aircraft industry. The manufacturers themselves united behind the Aircraft Manufacturer's Association (AMA) in order to rectify disputes over patent rights and to lobby the government. The AMA's most important accomplishment was the institution of a cross-licensing agreement under which all member companies were allowed to use patents of the others for a uniform fee. This agreement became of inestimable aid to the young American industry, because in the years 1903 to 1914, European producers had seized the technological initiative.

Inundated with military orders, American manufacturers went to work. In 1914, the 16 aircraft manufacturers listed by the U.S. Census produced only 49 planes. By 1918, the annual total had risen to 14,000.[1] More than 40,000 aircraft engines were also produced that year, in large part by automobile companies. Many of the airframe units were from European designs, such as Hispanos and DeHavillands. Thus, in the early days the United States was a net importer of airplane technology, and indeed, it was this importation that aided Americans in closing the technology gap.

The war boom attracted many entrepreneurs to the market who had never built airplanes before and who were driven out of the market soon after the armistice. Within a matter of days after the signing of the treaty, $100,000,000 in aircraft contracts had been canceled.[2] This experience represented the first violent cycle in sales—a boom-and-bust cycle that was to become characteristic of the industry. With the absence of any significant export or commercial market, production by American manufacturers collapsed to a not-so-grand total of 263 airframes in 1922. The armed forces exacerbated an already desperate situation by reselling surplus aircraft and engines in the domestic market.

It would be a misconception, however, to imagine that the industry returned to its prewar state. Although demand fell sharply, it was considerably higher than in the earlier era. More to the point, the industry had the triple advantage of profits earned during the war, a new technology, and most importantly, a government convinced of the airplane's efficacy as an instrument of defense.

The Trend Toward Geographic Concentration

It was during these years that the industry's trend toward geographic concentration began. The deliberate economic decision of Donald Douglas to locate the new Davis-Douglas company in Santa Monica was the first step in this process. Douglas first chose the Los Angeles area and then sought backing and factory space. This location decision was possible, because in the aircraft industry accessibility to materials and markets was a negligible factor in determining location, and capital was usually procurable from local sources, at least in a company's early days. The predominating factors were a climate that permitted year-round flying and an adequate supply of skilled and semi-skilled labor.[3]

By 1940, 45 percent of the nation's airframe manufacturing facilities were located in southern California,[4] while other manufacturers were gravitating toward the Northeast. Just as the airframe manufacturers were attracted to the West by superior flying conditions, propeller and engine firms were attracted to the Northeast by its industrial heritage and abundant supply of skilled craftsmen. In *New England: A Study in Industrial Adjustment*, R. C. Estall remarked, "Few other areas could provide a body of labor as skilled in metalworking trades of such variety together with comparable facilities for the manufacture of specialized parts and materials to the close tolerances required for aircraft engines."[5] Indeed, it was in New England that the American metalworking industry began, and subsequently grew to maturity. Eventually, this migratory trend became somewhat of a self-fulfilling prophecy; as more firms located in the area, a labor force grew up around them that had been trained and employed by the aircraft industry itself, offering agglomeration economies to new market entrants as well as to existing firms. Two New England firms that developed at this time were Sikorsky Aero Engineering Company of Stratford, Connecticut, and Pratt & Whitney of East Hartford. Their stories are not atypical of the time.

Sikorsky was incorporated in March 1923 by a small group of Russian refugees led by Igor Sikorsky. Most of the capital for this venture came from Arnold Dickinson, a Massachusetts businessman. A year later, Pratt & Whitney Aircraft was founded by Frederick B. Rentschler and Dr. George J. Meade. Rentschler formerly had been the president of Wright Aeronautical Company before resigning in a dispute with the board of directors. Rentschler and Meade's plan was to develop and manufacture radial, aircooled aircraft engines. Most of their original venture capital came from the Niles Tool Company of Connecticut. Niles, which owned the Pratt & Whitney Machine Tool Company of East Hartford, leased its idle Pratt & Whitney Machine Tool plant to the new concern. Rentschler retained the name because of its "established reputation for mechanical precision." In addition to the attraction of an existing idle plant, the existence of an abundant supply of skilled labor inherited from the earlier concern played a key role in attracting the new aircraft firm to East Hartford.

Pratt & Whitney launched its operations with a $90,000 sale of six experimental engines to the U.S. Bureau of Aeronautics. One of these engines was the famed "Wasp" engine. The qualities of the Wasp (light in weight and powerful in performance) were evident enough for the Navy to place an immediate order for 200 engines even though production costs for this quantity of a novel design were very uncertain. In placing their orders both the Army and Navy had embarked upon their first peacetime procurement programs involving both development and production contracts.

In the civilian sphere, the Air Mail Act of 1925 empowered the U.S. Postmaster General to contract for airmail service. The act came as a direct result of the recommendations of the Morrow Board, an advisory body convened by President Coolidge to investigate America's air power needs. This milestone was significant, as it heralded the first glimmerings of at least a quasi-commercial demand, and exemplified the government's growing willingness to subsidize the airlines and aircraft manufacturers.

Airmail contracts were awarded on the basis of time-honored competitive bidding, but the method of awarding military contracts was unconventional and clearly more entertaining. Air races became the accepted proving ground for military prototypes, and they included both foreign and domestic entries. Although competition among nations was merely for sport, rivalries garnered sales as well as glory for the victor. By the late 1920s, the Americans began to win a great many of the races as U.S. aeronautical technology rose to preeminence. Competition was so fierce for the limited number of contracts that profits were reinvested exclusively in research and development. Major technological breakthroughs were manifold, including the stretched-metal fuselage skin, the tear-drop wing, the swept wing, the aileron, and the variable pitch propeller blade.

Charles Lindbergh's transatlantic flight, in conjunction with the institution of airmail service and renewed government procurement, lent the industry new respect on Wall Street. The aircraft companies soon became the glamour stocks of the financial community, and investment money began to pour in. Lindbergh's flight occurred in May 1927 in a plane powered by a Wright "Whirlwind" engine. A month before, the company's stock had been selling at 25, but by December 1927, it had more than tripled in value, going to 94¾; a year later it reached 245.[6]

Formation of the Conglomerates

Although many stocks turned in impetuous performances during those two years, the value placed on the aircraft company stocks by the market was at best questionable. Predatory practices were common to the financial world of that time. A flurry of corporate mergers and acquisition activity occurred, and when it ended, three conglomerates emerged to dominate the industry: Boeing, Avco, and General Motors.

Avco, or Aviation Corporation, made acquisitions, including Detroit Aircraft, Lockheed, and Consolidated Vultee.

The General Motors sphere of influence was a result of a merger with North American Aviation. North American had under its control Curtiss-Wright, Wright Aeronautical, and Sperry Gyroscope; General Motors had absorbed Fokker, Bendix, Allison, and Dayton-Wright.

Boeing was reorganized in 1928 as United Aircraft and Transport Corporation and merged with Pratt & Whitney Aircraft. Early in 1929, Hamilton Aero Manufacturing Company, Chance-Vought, and Hamilton Metalplane Company were added to the conglomerate. In April of that year it acquired Stout Air Lines. In September, Sikorsky Aviation Corporation and Standard Steel Propeller Corporation were added, and in October, Stearman Aircraft Company and Northrup.

Hamilton Aero had been located in Milwaukee and Standard in Pittsburgh before their operations were merged in 1920. The new entity consolidated its operations in Pittsburgh, but it was bought out by the conglomerate UA&T in 1929. In 1931 operations were relocated to East Hartford, allegedly because of "labor trouble" in Pennsylvania as well as a desire to centralize production (P&WA was already located there).

These three conglomerates accounted for virtually all of the market supply in airframes and engines until the middle of the Depression. The U.S. government, which essentially *was* the market during this era, fostered this concentration either wittingly or unwittingly by means of production and air mail contracts. In the case of aircraft procurement, two of these large entities were awarded over 80 percent of all production contracts from 1927 to 1933 (see Table 2.1). Military demand was confined to 10 companies, which received roughly 90 percent of this business.[7] In reviewing the state of the industry, the Standard Statistics Company concluded, "the other 286 companies manufacturing planes have almost no participation in this stable [i.e., government] business."[8] Concentration among airmail carriers was also striking: 90 percent of the contracts were awarded to three firms.[9] Thus, aircraft manufacturing and air transport became the most "sheltered" industry in the nation.

Charges of profit gouging and unfair competition in awarding airmail contracts led to speculation about the fairness of the airmail business. As a result, several congressional investigations were initiated with that of the Crane Committee notable among them. In 1934 all airmail contracts were abruptly canceled. The Army Air Corps flew the mail temporarily while the Crane Committee considered the pattern of dominance among the prime contractors. The main issue was the dovetailed nature of transport service and manufacturing concerns. Since the conglomerates filed consolidated income statements, bookkeeping losses in one division could be charged against the income of others. As a result, the government paid more for purchases because of unprofitably managed mail routes.

Congressional scrutiny resulted in both the Vinson-Trammel Act and a second Air Mail Act in 1934. Vinson-Trammel limited the profit rates suppliers could realize on sales to the government, while the new Air Mail Act ruled that manufacturing concerns must divest themselves of their transport activities. Direct antitrust action ensued as a result of this legislation, and the burgeoning sphere of conglomerate influence was effectively reduced. Subsequent divestiture occurred as follows:

- United Aircraft was divided into three separate entities: two manufacturers, Boeing and United Aircraft, and one transport company, United Airlines. United Aircraft maintained control of Pratt & Whitney, Hamilton-Standard, Chance-Vought, and Sikorsky.
- General Motors/North American separated into Eastern Airlines, Trans World Airlines, and North American Aviation.
- Aviation Corporation split into Avco and American Airlines.

Table 2.1   Plane and Engine Sales, 1927–1933

Companies	Sales to Navy	% of Sales to Navy	Sales to Army	% of Total Army Sales	Commercial Sales	% of Total Commercial Sales	Total Sales	% of Total Sales
1. UA&T (Boeing, Chance-Vought, Pratt & Whitney)	$33,212,890	48.4	$16,971,553	29.3	$28,056,208	48.0	$78,240,651	42.3
2. Curtiss-Wright (Curtiss, Wright, Keystone)	15,707,937	22.9	29,047,653	50.2	26,813,517	45.9	71,569,107	38.7
United and Curtiss Totals	48,920,827	71.3	46,019,206	79.5	54,869,725	93.9	149,809,758	81.0
3. Douglas	4,551,018	6.7	9,886,605	17.1	1,412,790	2.4	15,850,413	8.6
4. Glenn Martin	9,886,605	14.4	none	—	none	—	9,895,605	5.4
5. Great Lakes	2,418,307	3.5	33,686	.1	905,719	1.5	3,357,712	1.8
6. Consolidated Aircraft	2,347,622	3.4	1,960,010	3.3	1,118,231	1.9	5,425,863	2.9
7. Grumman	452,195	.7	none	—	153,492	.3	605,687	.3
Total of Independents	$19,664,747	28.7	$11,880,301	20.5	$3,590,232	6.1	$35,135,280	19.0
Total of All Companies	$68,585,574	100.0	$57,899,507	100.0	$58,459,957	100.0	$184,945,038	100.0

SOURCE: G. R. Simonson, *The History of the American Aircraft Industry* (Cambridge, Mass.: MIT Press, 1968), p. 86.

This division set the stage for the corporate structure of the modern day. In New England, United Aircraft Corporation consolidated its East Coast manufacturing holdings in Connecticut, specifically in the Hartford and Bridgeport areas. The Pratt & Whitney division remained in East Hartford, while the newly consolidated Hamilton-Standard division occupied a site in Windsor Locks. Sikorsky reorganized in a new plant in Stratford, Connecticut, where it began to build the successful S-38 twin-engined amphibian aircraft. Modifications ultimately led to the production of the S-42 "Sikorsky Clipper," otherwise known as the Pan Am Flying Boat.

United Aircraft, however, eventually came to consider the Sikorsky operation too costly to continue. It abandoned flying boats in 1938, but chose to finance Sikorsky's attempt to design a workable helicopter. Chance-Vought originally moved to Hartford, "but subsequently settled in Bridgeport when it was decided that the United Aircraft Corporation was over-concentrating its facilities in the Hartford area."[10] Airframe manufacture remained on the West Coast, stretching from Long Beach, California, to Seattle, Washington, with pockets in the Mid-West and the Northeast. This was how the industry was arrayed on the eve of World War II.

World War II Expansion

The 1930s were a time of intensive aircraft engine development. Late in the decade, military procurement officers decided to direct development efforts toward liquid-cooled models. This decision was initially disastrous for Pratt & Whitney, which had concentrated its research upon air cooling. The firm was on the verge of closing down as a result of this government decision when the immediate defense needs of France and Britain filled the breach. As had been the case since the early 1920s, when government production and mail contracts constituted almost the entire market, government decisions determined the success or failure of even the largest producers.

The reorganization of the aircraft industry during the 1930s strengthened the existing location pattern of the industry. The trend toward geographic concentration begun by Douglas Aircraft in 1920 reached full flower by the latter part of the decade. By

1937 California's sales of aircraft products led all other states with $51 million; New York was a distant second with sales of $15 million.[11] By 1939, 46 percent of all airframe production floor space was on the West Coast, with 24 percent in the Northeast.[12]

Engine and propeller production was even more geographically concentrated with over 80 percent of the production floor space for these two products located in Connecticut and New Jersey. Only the Wright Aeronautical Division of the Curtiss-Wright Corporation, located in Paterson, New Jersey, ranked with P&W in the production of aircraft engines. In propeller manufacture the only major producer apart from Hamilton-Standard was the Curtiss-Wright Propeller Division in Clifton, New Jersey. The importance of the availability of skilled and semi-skilled labor in these regions played a key role in promoting this trend.

The war actually began in 1938 for the American aircraft industry, when the martial fervor in other nations began to precipitate into open warfare. By this time the demand for aircraft had been so widely differentiated that, in contrast to World War I, fighters, bombers, transports, and trainers were all of different design. Export of these items was somewhat of a problem in 1938 because of the Neutrality Act and the pervasive isolationist mood of America. Even so, weaponry orders began to accumulate from China, Revolutionary Spain, Great Britain, and France. When the Neutrality Act was finally repealed the accumulation turned into a flood; the day afterward, it has been said, the stocks of munition companies were among the highest fliers on the stock market.

The succession of events leading to the industry's total mobilization culminated in Germany's aerial blitz of Britain. President Roosevelt requested the manufacture of 50,000 planes over the next year. In 1939 only 5,856 planes had been produced, of which 2,195 were military aircraft.[13] Roosevelt's request was consequently more startling than realistic, for plant space available at the time was far short of that needed for such an output. Furthermore, companies were not willing to expand on the strength of speeches, and they refused to be burdened with what would be unusable plant capacity after the war. The experience of the post–World War I industry collapse had not been forgotten.

To meet the demands of defense contractors, most of the new expansion in production facilities was therefore financed by the government. The corporation income tax code was amended to allow new aircraft manufacturing facilities to be depreciated over five years. When this almost immediately proved inadequate by itself, the government's main effort at capacity expansion turned to the use of the Emergency Plant Facilities (EPF) contract. This was an agreement whereby the manufacturer first financed construction through the private money market or the Reconstruction Finance Corporation (RFC). The government then reimbursed the manufacturer over a five-year period, after which it either assumed title to the plant or sold it back to the manufacturer. The EPF arrangement proved to be cumbersome and mutually unsatisfactory. For the balance of the war, it was replaced by a system whereby the RFC established a subsidiary, the Defense Plant Corporation, that built the new facilities itself and leased them to the aircraft firms.

General Electric was one of the many firms that took advantage of the arrangement. Its facility in Everett, Massachusetts, for example, was built in 1941 by the U.S. government, which retains ownership to this day. Many of the new plants that were constructed were required to be located inside a so-called defense zone (that is, at a distance from both coasts) to ensure safety from enemy attack. This strategic consideration was one factor responsible for a temporary reversal of the increased geographic concentration that had been experienced during the 1930s.

While the new plants were erected rapidly and others were converted to wartime use, skilled labor was as hard to find as it had been easy during the 1930s. Much of the trained labor force was being conscripted for military service, and other major defense industries were competing for the remaining workers. This consideration became the major non-strategic constraint on plant location during the war. Not only did communities have to be found where the labor force was not preempted by another major industry, but considerations such as housing, energy, and transportation also had to be taken into account. Pressure upon labor and production facilities in the Hartford, Connecticut, area became so severe that the manufacture of many aircraft parts and sub-assemblies was established elsewhere. Government plants were built for Pratt & Whitney at Southbridge and Willimantic, Connecticut, and at Springfield, Massachusetts, while Hamilton-Standard occupied idle mills in Pawtucket, Rhode Island, and New London, Connecticut. The use of these facilities, however, was not to last long. The original plants in Hartford resumed normal operations after the war, and the outlying areas quickly lost all interest in aircraft and parts production.

To expedite the war effort, jobs were filled by the young, the aged, the infirm, but especially and most successfully, by the nation's women. The government was forced to provide general training and specific skills, for only with a skilled labor force could required production levels be maintained. A whole generation of skilled machinists was trained in this way, more than enough to fill most industry needs for several decades. Moreover, because of the need to produce vast quantities of airplanes with an initially unskilled labor pool, it was also necessary to redesign production techniques to a more continuous mode.

Subcontracting was not widespread before the war, and licensing agreements were generally nonexistent. Both of these methods of production were widely adopted during the war, however. Pratt & Whitney engines, to cite one example, were built by Ford, Buick, Chevrolet, and Nash. After 1940, contracting procedures also changed as the government's desire for massive output became manifest. Prior to the war, most contracting was on a fixed-cost basis. If costs exceeded those in the package proposal, contractors had to absorb the loss. At a time when costs were being subjected to severe inflationary pressure, the government recognized this type of contract as wholly unrealistic. This attitudinal change led to a gradual shift in procurement policy, and in time the cost-plus-fixed-fee contract predominated. This arrangement guaranteed firms a fixed profit because the government agreed to pay for any cost increases during the course of the contract.

Most historians agree that the American industrial effort was the pivotal factor in World War II, and the aircraft industry was the cornerstone of that effort. During the conflict, some 300,000 airplanes, 800,000 engines, and 700,000 propellers were built in America. In the process, the industry rose from forty-fourth in dollar value of output in 1939 to first in 1944.[14] Such figures are even more informative when compared to production in other countries. (see Table 2.2).

World War II was clearly the force behind the greatest expan-

Table 2.2　Production of Military Aircraft of Four Major Belligerents

Year	Germany	U.K.	Japan	U.S.A.
1939	8,295	7,940	4,467	2,141
1944	39,807	24,461	28,180	96,318

SOURCE: W. F. Craven and J. L. Cates, "Men and Planes" as cited in John Bell Rae, *Climb to Greatness: The American Aircraft Industry, 1920–1960* (Cambridge, Mass.: MIT Press, 1968), p. 172.

sion in the history of the industry, and it fostered an impressive array of technological advances. The first practical design of a helicopter, Igor Sikorsky's VS-300, was test flown in early 1939. Sikorsky was one of three manufacturers who supplied the Army Air Corps with experimental models during the war, having 151 of them accepted. Platt-Lepage Aircraft Company of Eddystone, Pennsylvania (2), and Nash-Kelvinator Corporation of Detroit (201) were the others.[15] Nash-Kelvinator, however, was a licensee of the Sikorsky Division.

By the end of the war, the only operational jet fighter belonged to Germany, but American and British research was not far behind. NACA had established a committee on jet propulsion in March 1941 under the chairmanship of W. F. Durand. The Durand Committee promptly awarded development contracts to the nation's principal manufacturers of turbines: General Electric, Westinghouse, and Allis-Chalmers. In a tactical move, the committee refused to provide Pratt & Whitney with similar funding, ostensibly to prevent diversion of resources from conventional engine production. General Electric was apparently in an advantageous position because its experience with building turbo-superchargers for the war effort proved invaluable in overcoming some of the difficulties associated with gas turbines. As it was, GE was responsible for the I-A engines in the first American experimental jet plane, the Bell XP-59A. This milestone, made possible by the government-sponsored research at Lynn, Massachusetts, put GE into a clear lead in the field of jet engine production. Following the war, General Electric (together with Westinghouse) largely monopolized the production of jet engines, and the Lynn plant became well established before traditional engine firms could gain a foothold in the market. This "monopoly" deteriorated in subsequent years, however, and Pratt & Whitney assumed a dominant role in the industry.

While new engine development was occurring on the East Coast, the airframe manufactures were redesigning their planes in California and Washington. Heavy bomber designs to replace Boeing's B-17 were invited by the War Department in 1939. Consolidated designed and built the B-24 Liberator, followed in quick succession by North American's extraordinarily successful B-25 and Martin Aircraft's B-26 Marauder. Fighter production, which had centered on the P-40 in 1939, expanded to include Bell Aircraft's P-39 Airacobra, Lockheed's dual-fuselage P-38 Lightning, Republic's famous P-47 Thunderbolt, and North American's P-51 Mustang. The workhorse of the air fleet was the Douglas DC-3, renamed the C-54 for military purposes.

By the end of the war, North American had produced over 41,000 planes, followed by Convair, Douglas, Curtiss-Wright, Lockheed, Boeing, Grumman, Republic, and Bell[16] (see Table 2.3). The planes were capable of quicker acceleration, faster cruising and attack velocities, higher altitudes, greater payloads, more fire power, and longer flights. They bore little resemblance to the military planes that predated the war and began to take on the aerodynamic styling that would usher in the jet age.

The Beginning of the Post–World War II Period

When the outcome of the war became apparent, both the government and the industry began to consider ways in which to make the contract termination procedure as orderly as possible. The early planning and the incipient Cold War that followed made the inevitable demobilization smoother than that of 25 years earlier. As John Bell Rae notes in his excellent history of the aircraft industry:[17]

> *Procedures for orderly contract termination were adopted in 1943, and were adopted in the Contract Settlement of 1944. In order to avoid needless disruption of industry when military requirements changed or disappeared, the contract termination process attempted to: 1) phase out war contracts as gradually as conditions permitted, 2) prevent manufacturers and their subcontractors from being left with vast quantities of unusable inventory, and 3) provide some assistance in reconverting to peacetime production.*

Nevertheless, by the end of 1945 contracts amounting to over $21 billion had been canceled. Only 16 airframe plants out of 66 remained in operation. Between 1944 and 1947, industry sales dropped by 90 percent.[18] In January 1944, 23 aircraft engine firms were in operation; by December 1945 this number had dwindled to 5.[19] Dramatic though these figures may be, the measurement of plant space can be deceptive, for some of the remaining production capacity was idle or semi-idle. Employment figures indicate a more radical contraction. In November 1943 total industry employment numbered 1,460,000; by March 1946, only 219,000 were employed.[20] In New England, industry employment, which

Table 2.3   Aircraft Production by Firm, 1940–1945

Company	Production by Number of Units
North American	41,188
Convair	30,903
Douglas	30,696
Curtiss-Wright	26,154
Lockheed	18,926
Boeing	18,381
Grumman	17,428
Republic	15,603
Bell	13,575
Eastern Aircraft Division, General Motors	13,449
Martin	8,810
Chance-Vought	7,890
Ford	6,791
Goodyear	3,940

Company	Production by Airframe Weight *(thousands of lbs)*	Percent of 5-Year Grand Total
Douglas	306,573	15.3
Convair	291,073	14.6
Boeing	226,447	11.3
North American	210,913	10.5
Lockheed	180,118	9.0
Curtiss-Wright	136,091	6.9
Martin	126,970	6.3
Ford	123,076	6.2
Republic	75,893	3.9
Grumman	73,767	3.7
Bell	53,037	2.7
Eastern	47,869	2.4
Chance-Vought	28,952	1.4
Goodyear	13,668	0.7
All other plants	101,136	5.1
Grand total—all plants	1,995,613	100.0

SOURCE: W. F. Craven and J. L. Cate, "Men and Planes," as cited in John Bell Rae, *Climb to Greatness: The American Aircraft Industry, 1920–1960* (Cambridge, Mass.: MIT Press, 1968), p. 168.

had risen from a 1938 level of 7,000 workers to a peak of 85,000 in February 1944, fell to 21,000 in 1945.[21]

Reduction of output was not the only significant change that occurred after the war. The massive geographical shift to the nation's interior that occurred in 1940 was reversed; if output was to be cut by 90 percent, the manufacturers preferred to produce the remainder on the coasts. This shift was universally anticipated and, not unexpectedly, regional political coalitions clashed in a dispute that presaged the current Sunbelt versus Frostbelt debate:[22]

> *A campaign for greater dispersal of the aircraft industry was energetically conducted by the Mid-Continent Industrial Council, composed of business and political leaders in Texas, Oklahoma, Kansas, Nebraska, South Dakota, Iowa, Missouri and Arkansas. It was opposed by the All-America Defense Association, representing the Pacific Coast, the Rocky Mountain states, the Great Lakes area, New England and New York. This agitation had very little effect. . . . Aircraft manufacturers, like any others, were reluctant to abandon existing facilities unless there was compelling reason to do so. . . .*

A certain amount of permanent dispersion did occur as a result of the war, but not enough to refute the rule. Boeing moved a portion of its operations to Wichita, and in another, far more extensive move, United Aircraft's Chance-Vought Division moved from Bridgeport, Connecticut, to the Dallas area. One author called this particular move "one of the most spectacular migrations in recent industrial history"; in all, some 1,500 people, 2,000 machines, and 50 million pounds of equipment were involved.[23] The relocation was chiefly a strategic matter. Prior to 1948 four major aircraft manufacturers were located in western Connecticut (Pratt & Whitney, Sikorsky, Chance-Vought, and Hamilton-Standard—all United Aircraft firms), while an additional two companies (Republic Aviation and Grumman Aircraft) were situated on Long Island. All of them were within 70 miles of Bridgeport, which put a severe strain on the area's labor force. Moreover, Chance-Vought and Grumman were the chief manufacturers of naval fighters, and naval authorities were anxious to break up this geographical concentration of production.

R. C. Estall, an expert on New England development, notes additional reasons for the Chance-Vought move:[24]

> *When a war-time plant in Dallas came up for lease in 1946, the Navy raised the issue of relocation with Chance-Vought. Of the two naval aircraft producers in the Long Island–Bridgeport area,*

Vought was the more likely to consider a move at that time. Its plant outside Bridgeport was proving restrictive, and its airport facilities were too cramped for the fast jets that were being produced in increasing numbers. Dallas offered a large plant, a big adjacent airfield, 90 percent flying time (compared to 75 percent in Connecticut), lower upkeep costs, especially in fuels, and a safer area for the testing of new planes. After about two years of negotiation and preparation, Chance-Vought moved, assisted financially by the Federal Government.

Such a move, however, was unique in the industry. With huge amounts of physical capacity invested in one site, mobility was largely precluded. As it happened, United Aircraft divested itself of Chance-Vought in 1954, finding, as General Motors had, that the organizational structure required for airframe manufacturing was totally different from that required for engine production.

The trend of reversion to prewar geographical locations dominated all other moves. Glenn Cunningham, an economic geographer, observed:[25]

The 1950 industry, after shrinking to about one-eighth the size of the 1944 industry, necessarily displayed a greatly altered pattern of distribution. Fewer regions, states, and metropolitan districts as producing units, greater concentration, and reduced rank of most of the interior area, summarize the principal variations. . . . The industry is located in the same seven regions as in 1940 but they appear in somewhat shuffled order except for the Pacific region, in first place in both years. New England has risen from fourth to third, and the West South Central from seventh to fourth.

As might be expected, the public debate over the geographical "reconcentration" was bitter, but the industry remained adamant in its plans to return to prewar locations. *Aviation News*, a leading trade paper, printed the industry's reasons for the shift:[26]

The early aircraft plants were built in their present locations for eminently practical reasons, and the same reasons will apply with equal force in the postwar period. . . . Restricted operations will require that the companies utilize their least expensive plants to remain in areas where the proper labor supply is located, where tax problems have stabilized, where good peacetime housing is available, and where climate is particularly suited to aircraft production.

Truly inland and southern manufacturing plants such as Omaha, Wichita, Fort Worth and Marietta still are dependent upon the vulnerable mid-northern industrial section for materials, parts and supplies.

The industry reiterated the same points before a congressional subcommittee on the demobilization of the aircraft industry:[27]

(1) *Prewar locations offer natural advantages as a result of climate, weather conditions, availability of labor, and so forth.*

(2) *The companies in many cases have substantial investments in their home plants and experimental facilities.*

(3) *Executives, key personnel, engineers and production workers have family ties, including home ownership, in their prewar localities. As a result, they would be reluctant to move and in moving a company valuable people might be lost.*

It was clear that nothing could stop the reconcentration in aircraft industry assets or the relocation of plant sites.

In 1950 the industry employed 212,000 workers nationwide.[28] While California's grip on the manufacture of airframes remained virtually as strong in 1950 as in 1939 (40 percent of employment[29] and 45.4 percent of production floor space),[30] New England's hegemony over the engine market was undermined during the war, only to be recovered, and indeed, slightly strengthened by 1950. In 1940, 42.6 percent of all aircraft engine employment was in New England.[31] By 1944 it had fallen to 10.6 percent as licensees produced vast numbers of engines throughout the country. By 1950, however, 45.9 percent of all aircraft engine employment was back in the region.[32] In propeller manufacture, 63 percent of the nation's employment was in New England (virtually all in Connecticut) in 1940.[33] By 1944 the proportion had declined to 17.4 percent, and then rose again to 29.9 percent by 1950.[34] Thus by 1950 New England was once again among the leading areas of aircraft engine and propeller manufacture in the United States while the Pacific region remained strong in airframes.

The Korean Era

It is unlikely that the industry will ever again undergo an era as spasmodic as the years surrounding the two world wars, but it continues to exhibit the same general vicissitudes. The expansion of production for the Korean conflict was not nearly so pronounced as that which accompanied World War II, but it was significant nonetheless. For the first time America's defense forces encountered enemy jet-powered fighters in combat and almost complete re-equipment became necessary. By the end of the war the aircraft

industry had built over 15,000 jets.[35] Moreover, during the conflict, the helicopter was widely accepted as a useful craft with
valuable military applications, and as a result, production levels
increased accordingly. Military helicopter sales increased from 44
units in 1946 to 983 units in 1952, the peak year of the war.[36]
Sikorsky Aircraft was responsible for a large portion of this output.

With the new stimulus provided to the industry by the war,
nationwide aircraft employment quickly increased, reaching 822,000
in 1954.[37] Subsequent to demobilization, however, the type of
severe industry contraction that followed the previous two wars
did not occur. With the Cold War, America assumed a more
strategic role in international affairs, and the industry received
the military contracts implied by that role. General Hap Arnold,
Chief of the Army Air Corps at the end of World War II, set the
tone for the military jet age that would follow in an era of "peace."[38]

> *In two World Wars the aggressor has moved against other, peace-*
> *loving nations, hoping that the United States would remain aloof*
> *or that other nations could be defeated before this country's power*
> *on land, air, and sea could be brought to bear against him. Luckily,*
> *in each war there has been time for the mobilization of such power*
> *and the U.S. has been the determining factor in the defense of*
> *civilization. The lesson is too plain for the next aggressor to miss:*
> *the U.S. will be his first target.*
>
> *There will be no opportunity for our gradual mobilization, no*
> *chance to rely on the efforts of others. It is of the utmost importance*
> *that our first line of defense, in the air, must be manned and fully*
> *supplied with modern equipment. We must be able to provide for*
> *other parts of the national defense machine to mobilize and go into*
> *high gear. The U.S. must be the world's first power in military*
> *aviation.*

The aircraft industry would play a crucial role in the new era of
nuclear superpowers and what President Eisenhower called the
"military-industrial complex."

Endnotes

1. G. R. Simonson (ed.), *The History of the American Aircraft Industry* (Cambridge, Mass.: MIT Press, 1968), p. 23.
2. John Bell Rae, *Climb to Greatness: The American Aircraft Industry,
   1920–1960* (Cambridge, Mass.: MIT Press, 1968), p. 2.
3. *Ibid.*, p. 11.
4. *Ibid.*, p. 10.

5. R. C. Estall, *New England: A Study in Industrial Adjustment* (New York: Frederick Praeger Publishers, 1966), p. 158.
6. Simonson, p. 76.
7. *Ibid.*, p. 84.
8. *Ibid.*, p. 84.
9. *Ibid.*, p. 83.
10. Estall, p. 170.
11. Rae, p. 92.
12. *Ibid.*, p. 108.
13. *Ibid.*, p. 108.
14. *Ibid.*, p. 169.
15. *Ibid.*, p. 228.
16. *Ibid.*, p. 168.
17. *Ibid.*, p. 173.
18. *Ibid.*, p. 173.
19. Simonson, p. 185.
20. *Employment and Earnings Statistics for the United States, 1909–1968*, Bureau of Labor Statistics, U.S. Department of Labor, Bulletin No. 1312–6, August 1968.
21. Estall, p. 160.
22. Rae, p. 197.
23. Simonson, p. 190.
24. Estall, p. 163.
25. Simonson, pp. 197–202.
26. *Ibid.*, p. 205.
27. *Ibid.*, pp. 205–206.
28. *Ibid.*, p. 196.
29. *Ibid.*, p. 196.
30. Rae, p. 108.
31. Estall, p. 161.
32. *Ibid.*
33. *Ibid.*
34. *Ibid.*
35. Charles D. Bright, *The Jet Makers* (Lawrence, Kansas: Regents Press, 1979), p. 15.
36. Rae, p. 204.
37. Estall, p. 160.
38. Simonson, p. 178.

Chapter 3

INDUSTRY TRANSFORMATION AND PROSPECTS

During the 1950s, the aircraft industry entered the modern era. The industry's products underwent radical transformation, and the market structure of the industry assumed a new form. In the commercial sector, the jet engine replaced the piston engine. Although by 1958 the jet turbine was already an established innovation in the U.S. Air Force, it had not yet become current with the airlines. The dominant forms of civilian long-distance transportation were still ship and rail. The adoption of jet transport by the airlines revolutionized air travel by making it faster and more comfortable.

While the Boeing 707 and Douglas DC-8 harbingered the birth of an entirely new commercial market, the guided missile began to partially replace the airplane as a strategic weapon. In this instance, aircraft firms were forced to compete with new market entrants from the electronics and metal alloy industries. The older aircraft firms met with qualified success. Years of dealing with the Defense Department had provided them with the experience needed to respond to government contract requests. In time, these firms came to dominate the development and production of missiles as well as traditional airframes and engines.

The Development of Commercial Markets

The initial generation of commercial jet transports did not go into production until late 1958, and they were not universally used by the airlines until well into the 1960s. Early in the 1950s, when the prospect of developing such an airplane was first bandied about, only four American airframe manufacturers had the technical and financial resources necessary for such an undertaking: Convair, Lockheed, Boeing, and Douglas.[1] Some might add Grumman and North American to this list, but both of them decided that their experience and interest lay with military aircraft.

Boeing was the first American airframe manufacturer with a successful entrant in the commercial field—the 707. In addition to its heritage of large aircraft manufacturing, Boeing had developed the first American jet bombers, the B-47 and B-52. This experience afforded it the ability to estimate overall development costs, an invaluable advantage over the other companies. Development began in 1952, and the first prototype 707 flew in 1954; the same design subsequently went into production in both a military and commercial version. The first commercial jet transport of the production run was completed in October 1958. The military model was called the KC-135 Stratotanker. Overall, the program was extraordinarily successful, echoing the success of the first truly popular commercial airliner, the DC-3, introduced 20 years earlier. The 707 established Boeing's supremacy in the large airframe market.

Douglas, which had been supreme in piston engine aircraft, failed to begin early development of its DC-8 jet transport. Unsure of the market potential for turbine-powered transports, Douglas remained cautious until American Airlines committed itself in 1955 to a capital expenditure program of $400 million for its new jet fleet, placing an order with Boeing for 30 707s.[2] Although the DC-8 went into airline service only one year after the 707, this lag was sufficient to cost Douglas its premier position in the commercial transport market. Convair arrived even later in the jet marketplace with its "880," entering only after Boeing and Douglas had effectively preempted the field. Lockheed, deciding to stay out of the jet transport competition altogether, targeted the turboprop market instead with its eventually lucrative "Electra."

The number of firms with hands-on jet turbine experience and development resources, small to begin with, had decreased even further. By 1955 only two companies had the wherewithal necessary for construction of a large transport turbine: Pratt & Whitney and General Electric.

Throughout this period Pratt & Whitney dominated the large commercial jet engine market. The company had used its own resources to develop turbine production capacity during World War II, while General Electric had the advantage of government-sponsored research and development. During the 1950s Pratt & Whitney concentrated on the civilian market while GE, operating out of Lynn, Massachusetts, and Evendale, Ohio, produced primarily for the military. Pratt & Whitney was therefore in good position when Boeing and Douglas began their search for a commercial power plant. In 1953 the company's J-57 gas turbine engine powered the first aircraft to crack the sound barrier. The commercial version of the engine, the JT-3, was chosen as the power plant for the earliest 707s and DC-8s. By 1968 Pratt & Whitney had captured over 90 percent of this growing market, which GE had largely abandoned because it misjudged the potential of the civilian segment.[3]

Development of the Missile Market

The military market was also changing rapidly. For some aircraft firms it was simply a matter of changing along with it or sinking into oblivion because an ever-increasing portion of Defense Department resources was being spent on missilery. In the late 1950s, one Air Force spokesman stated, "As readily as missiles become operationally suitable, they will be placed into units to either completely or partially substitute for manned aircraft according to military requirements."[4] The correct nature of this forecast can be seen in the figures presented in Table 3.1. The overall ratio of missile to aircraft sales rose from 3.8 percent in 1950 to more than 60 percent in 1963. An even more drastic change in the

Table 3.1 Aerospace Industry Sales by Product Group ($ millions)

Year	Total Sales	Aircraft	Missiles	Missiles/Aircraft Ratio
1950	$ 3,116	$2,731	$ 105	3.8%
1955	12,411	9,781	1,513	15.4
1960	17,326	9,127	5,762	63.1
1963	20,670	9,747	6,003	61.6

SOURCE: Aerospace Industries Association, *Aerospace Facts and Figures 1978/1979*, p. 12.

composition of military sales was experienced by several individual manufacturers. Lockheed's ratio of missiles to military sales, for example, grew from 2.2 percent in 1957 to 77.9 percent in 1960.[5]

There was no particularly compelling reason for the eventual domination the aircraft industry exercised over missile technology. According to R. C. Estall, "It is by no means a matter of natural progression to move from the manufacture of aircraft and aircraft parts into the missile field."[6] Missilery was such a novel science that it required new, highly specialized facilities. To quote an official of the Aerospace Industries Association:[7]

> *Although quite a bit of the productive know-how the industry had acquired in building aircraft was applicable to missilery, manufacturing methods underwent a revolutionary change. Missile parts had to be assembled in dust-free, vibration-free plants under rigid temperature and humidity control. These devices had to be continually tested and retested while they were actually on the production line. Computer operated tools were required for the high precision machining needed for missiles parts.*
>
> *The industry found that its old plants were not suitable for conversion to missile manufacture; missile facilities had to be built from the ground up. So, while industry was retiring its old plants for lack of plane production, it had to provide new facilities for missiles.*

The new facilities had enormous capital requirements. From 1956 to 1961, a relatively slack sales period between the Korean and commercial sales booms, aircraft companies spent over $2 billion on missile production capacity.[8] During the same period their sales of military aircraft fell by 34 percent.[9]

Many observers at that time felt that firms with other distinctive competencies were better qualified for missile development and production than aircraft manufacturers. D. C. Eaton, a prominent industry analyst, argued that, "The airframe manufacturers can no longer lay any claim to any special position in the industry. Companies whose experience and growth has been in electronics are and will be equally, if not better, qualified to perform major system development."[10]

Another perspective, however, suggests that airplanes and missiles have fundamental similarities that lend themselves to technology transfer. Both products, for instance, need an airframe, a power plant, and a guidance system. Additionally, the aircraft industry already employed a requisite amount of scientific and engineering talent, all of whom were practiced in the design of weapons systems. A third advantage was the aircraft industry's long, cumulative store of experience in dealing with the government, and the government's confidence in their ability to execute contracts. The importance of this factor in procuring contracts cannot be overestimated.

Initially, newcomers to the defense industry secured a large portion of the nascent missile market. Aircraft firms netted only a 24 percent market share in the business.[11] When missile technology reached the stage of full-scale production, however, the advantages lay with traditional aircraft manufacturers. By 1961 the market share of the aircraft firms had grown to 75 percent, vastly exceeding that of electronics manufacturers.[12] During 1956 missile production constituted only 5.7 percent of the aircraft industry's total sales. Two years later the proportion had risen to 25 percent, and by 1961 to a full 44 percent.[13]

One step beyond the new missile technology was the space race. New England, already renowned for its jet engines, would play a critical role in this market as well. In the two years following the Soviet Union's 1957 Sputnik launch, the U.S. government spent over $2 billion for space and defense contracts in the Boston area alone.[14]

> What prompted the Government to prime the space pump in Boston was the area's one great resource: brains. In and around Boston are such institutions as Harvard, MIT, Boston University, Tufts, and Northeastern. In 1957, 190,000 scientists, engineers, and technicians were living in the area—one working person in every five. Education, long regarded as a pleasant ornament to the Boston scene, had suddenly become a major asset.
>
> By 1959 there were some 480 space-oriented companies in the area. MIT alone, through its professors and alumni, had a hand in setting up more than 100 companies.

Most of this proliferation occurred in the vicinity of the Route 128 "Golden Crescent," and among the firms that benefited were General Electric, Avco, Honeywell, and RCA. A similar boom was experienced by California. Throughout the early 1960s this additional component to the aerospace industry brought the sector to near full capacity, and business became, as one industry source put it, "almost too good." On top of Minuteman, Apollo, and the Cuban Missile Crisis, the Indochina war began to escalate, assuring additional years of prosperity for the aircraft industry. The Cold War and the missile gap had served to sustain the industry between Korea and Viet-Nam.

The Viet-Nam Era

The war in Viet-Nam was obviously of much smaller scope than World War II, and the correspondent expansion of military aircraft pales in comparison. But in its own way, given the circumstances, it was just as important. In 1963, five years before the peak war year, 1,970 military aircraft were produced.[15] By 1968 this total had risen to 4,440, and by 1973 it had fallen back to 1,372.[16] A great part of this expansion was made up of helicopters, which as a result of the Kennedy Administration's "limited warfare concepts" were used extensively for the first time in Viet-Nam. The versatility and unique capabilities of the helicopter so revolutionized ground warfare that the military bought them in record numbers. Between 1965 and 1970 the Pentagon spent over $3 billion in tripling the size of its helicopter fleet to 12,000 units and in replacing an average of 600 helicopters lost annually in the war.[17]

The military was not the only purchaser of helicopters during this period, however. Domestic and export sales of helicopters jumped to record levels. The world helicopter market grew so quickly that U.S. manufacturers were hardpressed to expand fast enough. Industry spokespersons became extremely optimistic about the future prospects for a greatly expanded helicopter market as well, voicing beliefs that an end to American involvement in Viet-Nam would greatly enhance civilian sales, since a large number of helicopter pilots would be released from military responsibilities and be available to private business.

By 1967 aircraft markets were burgeoning so much that both plant space and the supply of skilled labor were in short supply. Total employment in the industry swelled from 605,000 to 860,000 in less than three years.[18] Even before the Viet-Nam escalation there was little or no excess plant capacity, and it became evident to both manufacturers and state governments that expansion was in order. Several states, hungry for economic development, courted aircraft firms with such enticements as favorable lease arrangements, indirect financial assistance, and land and market surveys. To meet labor needs, Pratt & Whitney, for one, found it necessary to institute a 5:30 P.M. to 9:30 P.M. "moonlight" shift for workers from other industries.[19] On the West Coast, most Lockheed workers were working six 10-hour days per week during the summer of 1967, and some worked seven days per week.[20]

Nationwide, real annual gross capital expenditures per employee in the industry increased by 70 percent between 1964 and 1968; in New England investment grew by even more—78 percent.[21]

Predictably enough, labor costs soared because of overtime and training program expenses. The lack of managerial options in this area did not escape the notice of national union leaders from the International Association of Machinists (IAM), International Union of Electrical Workers (IUE), and the United Auto Workers (UAW). The traditionally higher pay scale in the automobile industry had long been a bone of contention for aerospace workers, even though the UAW represented both industries. In the winter of 1968 Walter Reuther declared that the various aerospace unions, acting cohesively, would seek auto and aerospace wage parity during the imminent contract negotiations. By the following August the unions exceeded that goal.*

Other problems faced the manufacturers during the boom years of the 1960s. Owing to the overheated state of the aerospace market, strategic raw materials were in short supply. A combination of long inventory lead times and scarce labor resulted in ever-lengthening order backlogs. Usually considered an indicator of the industry's well-being, these backlogs grew so long that they severely tried the patience of the commercial airlines, which were also booming and eager to expand. Manufacturers doing business with the government always fill military orders first in wartime. Such was the case with Pratt & Whitney; its lead time for commercial engines was so long in 1966 that some airline officials grumbled about the dearth of turbine manufacturers.[22]

Labor, finance, and raw material shortages notwithstanding, the industry enjoyed its greatest cyclical boom since the Korean War. From 1965 to 1968 sales rose by 32 percent, employment by 23 percent, and backlogs by over half.[23] Aerospace once again became the titan of U.S. industry; the industry's profits grew faster than all others, and it became America's greatest exporter and manufacturing employer. The government/commercial marketing mix during 1968, the peak war year, was 70 to 30. Fifty-seven percent of total sales were made to the Department of Defense and 13 percent to NASA.[24] Research and development contracts consti-

---

* Parity was not maintained for long, however. With the end of the Viet-Nam boom, aerospace workers once again fell behind the pay packages negotiated by the UAW in the auto industry.

tuted 18 percent of the total sales dollars[25] and 35 percent of all
U.S. government R&D expenditures.[26] It is ironic to note, however, that the helicopter industry, which was growing at a record
pace throughout the period, was not a beneficiary of this R&D
money. In fact, there were no new military R&D project funds
allocated for helicopters between 1965 and 1970.[27] One may spec-
ulate that the government's reasoning behind this paralleled its
decision during World War II not to provide Pratt & Whitney
with R&D funds for jet turbines: a desire to keep all essential
resources in the area of engine production and thus fulfill the
immediate needs of the military.

In 1968 few industries did poorly, and cyclical downturns from
these lofty peaks were inevitable. That of the aircraft industry was
forecast quite early in 1969, when *Forbes* observed in its New
Year's Day issue that the industry's profits were slipping. *Forbes*
also remarked somewhat tardily that the two primary market segments, commercial and military, were showing identical trends.[28]
In fact, they had been doing so for some time, and these segments
were finally troughing out simultaneously. At about the time of
the *Forbes* article, the delivery period for commercial transports
began to shrink, as did prices and the level of progress payments.
Progress payments are the payments a purchaser makes on a
portion of the total contract obligation while production is still in
progress. When these payments decline it is generally construed
as a sign of increased price competition.

Military de-escalation was, of course, immediately detrimental
to the aircraft industry, but the ending of the war *per se* may not
have been as detrimental to the industry as the political influence
that the war had on Congress. For years afterward, Congress no
longer appropriated funds for Defense Department budgets without first scrutinizing those requests. Between 1968, the peak war
year, and 1971, the year of the Kissinger "peace," industry sales
to the Department of Defense dropped 24 percent in current
dollars.[29] The downturn in the military helicopter segment was
especially severe. In fiscal 1966, the Pentagon had budgeted $1.2
billion for the purchase of 3,350 helicopters. By 1971 this amount
had dropped to $242 million for slightly more than 1,000 heli-
copters.[30] The space program was also sharply curtailed; industry
sales to NASA fell by 30 percent over the same period.[31] Still,
it was in the commercial market that the industry took its worst
drubbing. Between 1968 and 1971 jet transport sales dropped by

68 percent.[32] In short, the industry was once again in a state of near collapse. *Aviation Week and Space Technology*, the industry's foremost trade journal, opined that 1970 was "the gloomiest year in decades."[33]

The Post–Viet-Nam Period, International Competition, and Future Prospects

The precipitous decline in the industry was due in large part to two factors, the first being the simultaneous collapse of both the military and commercial market segments. The second was the growing political influence of environmentalists and Pentagon critics who were finally gaining their day in court. Commenting on the industry's social and political estrangement, Robert Hotz, an obviously alarmed *Aviation Week* editorialist, remarked, "We have been warning on these pages for three years of the mounting assault on technology by a strange coalition of political opportunists, disgruntled youth, ecologists, and advocates of the social welfare state."[34]

No matter how one might view this so-called assault, it was nonetheless true that the political environment was shifting. Armed with a cogent analysis of supersonic transport economics and research on ecological impacts, the environmental lobby was successful in eventually severing all federal funds for the SST. Defense Department critics, with the aid of popular anti-war groups, were equally successful in stopping the B-70 manned bomber program, and later in convincing the Carter Administration to reduce development funding for the B-1. Again it was political-economic factors that dominated the market.

The New European Competition

Meanwhile, European manufacturers, who had lost the technological lead in commercial jet transports after being the first in the air with the ill-fated Comet, began once again to challenge U.S. preeminence in aircraft technology. The British and French governments undertook development of the supersonic Concorde in the early 1960s and continued to develop it even after all hope of short-term profit had been abandoned. European leaders were apparently willing to suffer substantial economic losses if domestic manufacturing capacity could be reincubated, and if their own national firms could begin to produce import substitutes for the large number of U.S.-built aircraft being purchased.

To enter the market with competitive products, the Europeans found it necessary to share both risk and capital financing through the organization of multinational consortia. The spirit of cooperation that resulted in the French–English consortium that produced the Concorde began this trend that has grown stronger with time. The largest and strongest of the European organizations to emerge from this cooperation was a consortium of several nations (including France, West Germany, Great Britain, the Netherlands, and Spain) called Airbus Industrie. It developed and currently produces a European wide-body commercial transport— the A300—and is now readying a second transport—the A310— for the production stage.

It was actually in the late 1960s that Airbus Industrie convinced the French and German governments to finance a two-engine, medium-range, wide-body transport to compete against the American entries in that emerging market. The other members of the consortium were later persuaded to join the effort, and together they contributed $1 billion for research and development and an additional $1 billion for working capital. Given the organization's current degree of success in penetrating the world commercial aircraft market, it would seem that the financial risk the member nations undertook in the 1970s was well calculated.

The recent growth in the European industry, and the new order of economic and political forces ushered in by it, will clearly have growing ramifications for the U.S. segment of the industry. These forces, which have been at play for the better part of a decade, have already begun to alter significantly the supply side of the market through the promotion of more intense European–American competition, at least in airframes. Indeed, by 1978 Airbus Industrie had already captured nearly 20 percent of the global airliner market, two thirds of the way toward the organization's goal of a 30 percent market share in new aircraft.

Europe's erosion of the U.S. jet engine market has not progressed as far, however. Despite the nationalization of Rolls Royce and the growth of France's SNECMA (the Société Nationale d'Etude et de Construction de Moteurs d'Aviation, a French government-owned aerospace concern), the impact of this new competition on the aircraft engine industry is neither direct nor does it take the form of a significant rival to Pratt & Whitney or General Electric. This is perhaps true only because the Europeans have not focused their investment in power plant production. Rather the near-term impact will be felt in the form of increasingly shared production and the export of both jobs and technology.

More recently the fortunes of the entire industry have changed again. This is true in the commercial market, in the general aviation and helicopter sector, and finally in the military market as a result of stepped-up defense spending.

The Future Market for Commercial Transports

The early 1980s represent the third "re-equipment cycle" for the airlines. Beginning with the first equipment cycle, which commenced with the advent of the commercial jet transport in the late 1950s, each generation was embedded in a new technology responsive to economic pressures. The first was a response to the demand for long-distance, fast, and comfortable transportation. The second generation, which encompassed the development, production, and sale of the wide-bodied "jumbo" jets, emerged as a response to the growth in demand for passenger-mile capacity and overcrowded airlanes. Environmental pressures and the "energy crisis" are responsible for the latest generation of commercial transports.

The short-run demand for commercial airliners will likely be enormous during this buying cycle, for virtually the entire world's air fleet must be re-equipped with fuel-efficient, low-pollution, quieter aircraft. Recent sales of Boeing's 757 to Delta and American airlines may represent only the tip of the iceberg, for it has been estimated that no more than one quarter of the jet transports that were operating at the end of 1978 can comply with Environmental Protection Agency (EPA) standards for 1985. Moreover, the average fleet airliner is nearly ten years old and was built during an era of inexpensive and plentiful jet fuel. In a time of rapidly rising operating costs, caused in large part by continually increasing fuel prices, the airlines have found it necessary to replace many of their currently operating airplanes. Virtually all 707s and DC-8s will have to be retired in favor of the new generation of aircraft, as will many 727s, 737s, and 747s. Although some of these airplanes can be retrofitted with quieter and more fuel-efficient engines, many will be mothballed sooner than anticipated. This factor, along with the renewed expansion of the U.S. defense budget, promises a new boom in aircraft sales despite the uncertain economic conditions of the early 1980s. This trend is almost certain to be reinforced by expansions in the business aircraft and helicopter markets.

General Aircraft and Helicopters: Growth Markets

The commercial segment normally comprises 45 to 55 percent of the total aircraft sales volume. In addition to large transports, business and general aircraft are included in this segment, and sales of these airplanes may very well increase substantially if rural, low-density routes are abandoned by the commercial sector in response to airline deregulation.

Between 1970 and 1977 general aircraft sales rose by 132 percent, partly as a result of the increased popularity of recreational flying, but more so as the result of the proliferation of in-house transportation for the growing number of multi-unit and multinational corporations. Standard and Poor's analysis of this market segment states that:[35]

> In past years, shipments of general aviation aircraft usually had closely followed the business cycle, rising when corporate earnings increased and falling when they receded. There was usually a lag of about six months after the corporate earnings trend was apparent. Recently, however, a new variable has altered the pattern. Schedule reductions by major airlines, implementation of nationwide 55 mph speed limits for automobiles, and a very successful advertising campaign have resulted in the surge in general aviation that is unrelated to the pattern of corporate earnings.

Among other things, the growth in this market and in the private commuter airlines may signal the resurgence of the propeller industry.

Some of the factors that beneficially influence general aviation will also help boost commercial helicopter sales. It is now generally recognized that the new higher-airspeed civilian helicopters, incorporating increased range, lower life-cycle costs, and smoother and quieter performance, provide real competition to fixed-wing business aircraft. Sales will also be enhanced by the ever-broadening number of helicopter applications, many of which are related to situations in which time has a relatively high opportunity cost: ambulance service, fire fighting, and news reporting. Resource

Table 3.2   U.S. Helicopter Sales, 1970 and 1979

Year	*Units*			*Sales Volume ($ millions)*		
	Mili- tary	*Com- mercial*	*Total*	*Mili- tary*	*Com- mercial*	*Total*
1970	1,944	482	2,426	$694	$ 49	$743
1979	158	1,019	1,177	219	403	622

Source: Aerospace Industries Association, *Aerospace Facts and Figures 1980/81*, pp. 35, 40.

exploration and development, especially in oil, gas, and timber, is also seen as a major force in stimulating helicopter sales in the near future.

A glimpse of this market potential can be seen in recent sales data. Between 1970 and 1979, civilian helicopter sales rose from $49 million to $403 million with the total number of production units increasing 111 percent[36] (see Table 3.2). During the same period, moreover, commercial market sales grew from a mere 7 percent of military sales to a point where the market value in the commercial sector was nearly double that of the military sector, although the average military helicopter cost more than three times the average civilian rotorcraft.[37] The growth in this sector will undoubtedly continue through at least the mid-1980s.

The Domestic Military Market

The U.S. Defense Department's share of the total aerospace market declined steadily between the end of the Viet-Nam-induced military buildup and the beginning of the 1980s. In 1979 the Department of Defense accounted for 37 percent of all sales, down from a peak of 58 percent in 1967.[38] The 873 military aircraft produced in 1977 marked the first time in more than a quarter century that the number fell below 1,000. Because relatively high value fighter and attack aircraft made up most of the deliveries, however, the decline in dollar value was moderate. Fly-away value, excluding spares and support equipment, was $4.3 billion in 1977, down from $4.7 billion in 1976.[39]

Budget limits during the 1970s necessitated strategic policy changes at the Pentagon. The military, unable to re-equip and grow comprehensively as it would have liked, evolved a more selective weapons procurement policy. This policy called for a "high/low" force mix or, stated less cryptically, the purchase of only a few highly destructive, single-mission weapons, complemented by many more general-purpose, tactical arms.

This strategy, with its consequences for the aircraft industry, would perhaps have been fully implemented if it were not for a dramatic shift once again in political factors. Beginning in fiscal year 1980, the federal government reversed the trend toward a falling share for the Department of Defense in total budget authority, providing for a 2 to 3 percent increase in the Pentagon's real purchasing power, despite an inflation rate of 11 percent. The Iranian hostage crisis and then the Soviet Union's invasion of Afghanistan turned the Carter Administration and Congress in a much more hawkish direction. The fiscal year 1981 budget, as approved by Congress, included a $52.8 billion defense hardware authorization bill, unprecedented in magnitude for a peacetime budget.[40] The bill includes money for the MX missile system and a new generation of bombers to replace the B-52 fleet. The MX alone will cost between $30 and $50 billion over the decade. Nearly $17 billion was earmarked for military research, development, testing, and evaluation for what Senator John Stennis, the chairman of the Armed Services Committee, called "a new start . . . to the most modern weaponry that science can devise."[41] This budget is expected to boost the entire range of military products produced by the aircraft industry.

Moreover, despite a popular belief that the SALT II treaty would have limited nuclear proliferation and competition between the Soviet Union and the United States, the agreement, if ratified, would actually have allowed more missiles than ever before. SALT II would have allowed each side to develop one new intercontinental missile system. The terms of the unratified agreement also included a stipulation that granted the United States the right to develop a supersonic bomber, thus offsetting the "strike advantage" that the Backfire bomber yields to the Soviets.

The American aircraft industry will also continue to supply many conventional weapons to the Defense Department, primarily fighters. The department is in the midst of a program to refurbish both U.S. and NATO equipment. To this end the department is scheduled to purchase large quantities of five different aircraft: the F-14, F-15, F-16, F-18, and the A-10 attack plane. Pentagon aircraft procurement policy since the early 1970s has called for the purchase of many low-cost fighters and a smaller number of more advanced, expensive ones. Present fighter procurement plans adhere to this principle.

In addition, there is a potentially expanded foreign military market. American firms have been extraordinarily successful in exporting military planes to Western Europe, Japan, and the Middle East, and despite the change of regime in Iran, foreign sales are expected to continue to be brisk for at least the next five years. In 1978 military exports totaled $4.0 billion, up from $2.2 billion in 1976.[42] The $4.0 billion in military exports compares with $6.0 billion in foreign civilian transport sales. Included in the civilian total were $3.6 billion for complete aircraft and $2.1 billion for parts, accessories, and equipment. As a result, by 1978 military and commercial foreign aerospace sales contributed over $10 billion to the U.S. international trade balance.[43]

Nevertheless, in regard to this renewed boom in the industry stemming from the planned re-equipment of the commercial fleet and escalated defense spending, it is necessary to add a note of caution. The successful metamorphosis of the industry cannot be expected to mitigate any of the long-term volatility in the market or insulate firms or their employees from the fickle nature of defense spending, the instability of foreign governments, or downturns in the commercial market. The traditional insecurity will persist, therefore, in spite of the current optimism in the industry.

Summary

It is now clear that the period from 1980 to at least 1983 or 1984 will be a boom period for aerospace. The industry will enjoy substantial short-term growth in the commercial market and in domestic and foreign military sales. Sales and profits will grow nationally, with New England and the West Coast gaining their traditional share of the market.

Employment is the big question mark. New automated production techniques and the export of prime and subcontractor production to foreign countries pose real problems for workers in the industry. The transformation in the competitive structure of the aircraft sector and its consequences for the locus of actual production have been no less dramatic than the change in the design of the product. Indeed, the nature of markets and competition in aircraft is unique, and in large degree helps to explain the dynamics of the capital and labor markets in the industry. In the following chapters we explore these issues.

Endnotes

1. John Bell Rae, *Climb to Greatness: The American Aircraft Industry, 1920–1960* (Cambridge, Mass.: MIT Press, 1968), p. 206.
2. *Ibid.,* p. 207.
3. "Pratt and Whitney Feels the Pangs of Success," *Business Week*, August 6, 1966, p. 139.
4. G. R. Simonson, *The History of the American Aircraft Industry* (Cambridge, Mass.: MIT Press, 1968), p. 229.
5. *Ibid.,* p. 237.
6. R. C. Estall, *New England: A Study in Industrial Adjustment* (New York: Frederick Praeger Publishers, 1966), p. 168.
7. Simonson, p. 233.
8. *Ibid.,* p. 232.
9. *Ibid.,* p. 230.
10. *Ibid.,* p. 253.
11. *Ibid.,* p. 239.
12. *Ibid.,* p. 240.
13. *Ibid.,* pp. 229–238.
14. "Rocky Ride on Route 128," *Forbes*, September 1, 1965, p. 32.
15. Aerospace Industries Association, *Aerospace Facts and Figures 1978/1979* p. 36.
16. *Ibid.*
17. "Military Helicopters Get Chopped Down," *Business Week*, August 29, 1970, p. 58.
18. *Employment and Earnings Statistics for the United States 1909–1968*, Bureau of Labor Statistics, U.S. Department of Labor, Bulletin No. 1312–6, August 1968, p. 376.
19. "Washington Roundup," *Aviation Week*, October 10, 1966, p. 25.
20. "Aerospace Firms Leaning Heavily on Overtime," *Steel*, July 10, 1967, p. 90.
21. *Annual Survey of Manufacturers, 1964–1968*, Bureau of the Census, U.S. Department of Commerce.
22. *Business Week*, August 6, 1966, p. 139.
23. "Aerospace Sales Boom Breaks Success Barrier," *Iron Age*, July 25, 1968, p. 92.
24. *Aerospace Facts and Figures 1978/1979*, p. 24.
25. *Ibid.*
26. *Iron Age*, July 25, 1968, p. 92.
27. *Business Week*, August 29, 1970, p. 58.
28. *Forbes*, January 1, 1969, p. 138.
29. *Aerospace Facts and Figures 1978/1979*, p. 31.
30. *Ibid.*
31. *Ibid.*
32. *Ibid.*
33. Robert Hotz, "Outlook for 1971," *Aviation Week*, January 11, 1971, p. 9.
34. *Ibid.*

35. Standard and Poor's, "Aerospace Basic Analysis," *Industry Surveys*, December 1, 1977 (Section 2), p. A15.
36. *Aerospace Facts and Figures 1980/1981*, p. 35.
37. *Ibid.*
38. *Ibid.*, p. 14.
39. *Aerospace Facts and Figures 1978/1979*, p. 8.
40. "$52.8b OK'd for Defense," *Boston Globe*, August 27, 1980, p. 3.
41. *Ibid.*
42. *Aerospace Facts and Figures 1980/1981*, p. 115.
43. *Ibid.*

Chapter 4

MARKETS AND COMPETITION
IN THE AIRCRAFT INDUSTRY

The nature of the aircraft market and the forms of competition engaged in by airframe and engine producers are quite unique in the American economy. No other industry operates in a market in which the cost of developing a single new prototype is so immense that it can make or break a billion-dollar enterprise. Nor are there many economic sectors that operate in an environment in which international bartering and even foreign intrigue determine so openly the success and failure of individual firms. Indeed, the political–economic world that surrounds the aircraft industry is one of the most turbulent found anywhere. It is amidst this often chaotic backdrop that the industry has changed dramatically.

As the industry evolved from World War II, it became essentially oligopolistic. Literally hundreds of smaller competitors were driven from the market, leaving a few aircraft giants. Immense capital and R&D requirements provided a natural market entry barrier, making it almost impossible for new firms to join the industry. The cost of developing a single new engine or airframe was well beyond the resources of all but a few firms. Before the first production engine is delivered in 1984, for example, Pratt & Whitney will have spent over a billion dollars on the development, pre-production, and tooling of the JT10D turbojet, now renamed the PW2037. Few governments, let alone private firms, have the wherewithal for undertaking such a risky endeavor, one that industry spokesmen describe as a "bet your company" proposition.

Yet despite the high degree of market concentration fostered by the cost of product development, the aircraft sector has actually

become more competitive. In the international market, new factors such as co-production, joint ventures, and offset agreements
have played a major role in determining a firm's competitive
position. Contract imperatives involving guaranteed, on-time production performance, as well as the interchangeability of engine
configurations on new aircraft, have also led to a more active
rivalry between the primary manufacturers. Customer demand
for timely delivery has become such an important consideration
that it has induced prime contractors to build their own parallel
production facilities as insurance against production disruptions.
They have also resorted to multiple sourcing as a hedge against
possible delays in the delivery of critical airframe and engine parts
from their suppliers. These strategies, and the new forms of competition from which they emerged, have profoundly changed the
structure and, indeed, the nature of the industry.

Sales Concentration in the Airframe Sector

The struggle for market share within the airframe sector of the
industry resembles the children's game, "King of the Mountain."
At the end of World War II, Douglas so dominated the market
with DC-3s that it had over 95 percent of the American commercial
fleet.[1] Even as late as 1958, the year of Boeing's introduction of
the 707, Douglas-designed DC-3s, 4s, 6s, and 7s accounted for
almost half (48 percent) of all commercial aircraft in the country.
Yet Douglas' tardy introduction of fan jets permitted Boeing to
displace the former aircraft king from the lofty position it had
occupied since the 1930s. By 1965 Boeing was by far the dominant

Table 4.1   **Concentration of Fleets by Manufacturer, Selected Years,
1932–1965**

Year	Douglas	Boeing	Lockheed	Consolidated/ Convair	Other/ Foreign
1932	0.0%	19.0%	8.0%	0.8%	70.2%
1935	17.7	28.6	18.1	1.9	33.8
1940	77.8	10.4	11.2	0.0	0.6
1946	95.4	0.8	3.8	0.0	0.0
1950	68.7	1.9	12.2	13.0	4.2
1958	48.0	0.7	18.4	18.0	14.8
1965	26.8	36.2	17.6	11.7	7.7

SOURCE: Amarin Phillips, *Technology and Market Structure: A Study of the Aircraft
Industry* (Lexington, Mass.: D. C. Heath, 1971), p. 30.

producer, as it had been almost 30 years before in 1935. Douglas was down to 27 percent of the market compared to Boeing's 36.2 and Lockheed's 17.6 (see Table 4.1). The Seattle-based Boeing was responsible for over 90 percent of all new additions to the air fleet in 1964 and more than 50 percent in every year between 1962 and 1965. The 707s, and even more so the 727 trijets, dominated the air lanes.

The Commercial Airframe Market Since 1970

With the arrival of the wide-body era in the late 1960s, the competition between Boeing, McDonnell Douglas, and Lockheed was rekindled as the three aircraft manufacturers struggled to provide the airlines with a new generation of wide-body commercial transports. All three firms expended massive amounts on development, pre-production, and tooling so that they could get their products to the market first. Boeing won the competition, but just as it was preparing to launch its new 747, the market for commercial airliners collapsed as a result of the impending 1970–1971 recession.

The plunge in aircraft orders had a severe impact on the operations of all the planemakers. Boeing's earnings, for example, plummeted from $83 million in 1968 to $10 million the following year.[2] To save the company from possible bankruptcy, top management reduced the workforce from 105,000 in 1968 to 38,000 in 1971, which, of course, devastated the entire Seattle economy.[3] Nonetheless, when the recession lifted Boeing quickly recovered, its supremacy in the commercial air transport market intact. By the beginning of 1980, its 747 had captured nearly 43 percent of the world wide-body market. The DC-10 had 31 percent while Lockheed's L-1011 achieved 17.7 percent (see Table 4.2).

Table 4.2　World Fleet of Wide-Body Aircraft Delivered by December 31, 1979

Aircraft	*Number Delivered*	*Percentage of Total Delivered*
Boeing 747	414	42.9%
McDonnell Douglas DC-10	299	31.0
Lockheed L-1011	171	17.7
Airbus A-300	81	8.4
Total	965	100.0%

SOURCE: Merrill Lynch and Company as reported in Winston Williams, "The Pall Over a Plane: McDonnell Douglas and the DC-10," *New York Times*, May 11, 1980.

With the beginning of the new decade a third jet-age re-equipment cycle is under way. The segment for entirely new commercial transports, spurred by noise and pollution regulations, skyrocketing fuel prices, airline deregulation, and the demand for increased capacity, promises a major expansion period throughout much of the 1980s. Estimates of worldwide market demand for commercial aircraft over the 10-year period ending in 1990 range from $80 to $130 billion. In the hope of capturing a significant share of this enormous market, Boeing, McDonnell Douglas, and Lockheed have each targeted specific areas for market penetration. In this cycle, however, all three of them are hesitant to engage in head-to-head competition in the same market, given initial McDonnell and Lockheed losses in the last re-equipment cycle.

Boeing has again led the competition. It is preparing for the introduction of two entirely new aircraft that promise to be fuel-efficient substitutes for the aging 707/727 fleet. The new transports (the 757/767 series) will derive much of their efficiency from the use of lighter raw materials, a more aerodynamic "supercritical" wing design, and more efficient engines. Both new transports will be smaller than the current wide-body aircraft. The 767, a twin jet built for the medium-range market, is in the 200-passenger category, while the 757 is somewhat smaller, designed to seat approximately 160 to 170 people. In addition to the 757 and 767, Boeing had earlier planned to add another plane, the 777, to its new offerings. Early designs placed it in the 260-passenger category, but because initial market reaction was far from promising, the project has been given a low priority. In late 1980, large orders from both Delta and American airlines gave 757 sales a major lift.

Unlike Boeing, McDonnell Douglas does not have a totally new aircraft to introduce during the current re-equipment cycle, which is due in large measure to the fact that the company has still not broken even on its DC-10. In the late 1970s, citing market competition from the Boeing 767 and its belief that European airlines would buy European products (the Airbus A300 and A310 series), the company abandoned its plans to develop an all-new 200-passenger jet. The company instead pinned its hopes on developing a plane to compete with the 757. At first the firm planned to build an advanced-technology medium-range (ATMR) transport. In mid-1980, however, Douglas announced that both technical and market assessment for the ATMR program would not be completed before mid-1981. Industry analysts differ widely in their opinions as to whether or not McDonnell Douglas will undertake the project. Some estimate that it would cost the company nearly $2 billion to develop the ATMR, and for a company with $2.6 billion in assets, it would indeed be a classic "bet your company" proposition.

In its place, the company decided to update its DC-9, developing the Super 80 derivative that it hopes will capture a significant share of the market for fuel-efficient and quieter aircraft. Despite the fact that the Super 80 will arrive on the market before the 757, the delay in building an ATMR appears to be similar to Douglas' hesitation in beginning development of the DC-8. This miscalculation cost Douglas its premier position in commercial aircraft manufacturing. Some experts maintain that without the ATMR, and despite the Super 80, the firm will eventually fall out of the commercial marketplace altogether. Company executives are said to be unwilling to let that happen.

McDonnell Douglas' current crisis stems largely from the adverse publicity surrounding crashes of its DC-10 aircraft in Chicago, Mexico City, and Antarctica. The rapid decline of public confidence in the plane may cause the loss of a significant number of potential DC-10 sales. In fact, new firm orders declined from 24 in the first half of 1979 to just 6 in the first half of 1980.[4] Moreover, several carriers, including American Airlines and Alitalia, were quick to cancel options on the plane. The difficulties involving the DC-10 not only impaired sales of that aircraft, but also may have damaged the prospects for future products such as a potential ATMR and a possible stretched version of the DC-10. This situation would undoubtedly make it increasingly difficult for the company to remain a major factor in the commercial aircraft market in the decades ahead.

Lockheed continues to rank third behind Boeing and McDonnell Douglas for market share in commercial air transport. When the wide-body era began in the late 1960s, Lockheed and Douglas were battling to produce a wide-body jet to compete directly against the 747. Lockheed's L-1011 Tristar offered more in terms of new and innovative technology than its rival's DC-10, but delayed introduction of the plane, caused by the bankruptcy of Rolls Royce, its engine supplier, caused many potential buyers to choose the Douglas Aircraft instead.

Even as Lockheed recovered from the financial difficulties that almost resulted in the company's bankruptcy in the early 1970s, the L-1011 program continued to lose money for the company. L-1011 losses for the first half of 1980 alone reached $128.3 million.[5]

Lagging sales in recent years (no aircraft orders in 1975 and only 31 between 1976 and 1978)[6] caused Lockheed to nearly drop out of the commercial market. Following Douglas' difficulties with the DC-10, however, Lockheed experienced a significant increase in demand for its L-1011, spurred in large measure by the introduction of its derivative L-1011-500, a shortened long-range version of the aircraft. Pan Am placed firm orders for 12 of the planes, with options to purchase an additional 14, placing the number of L-1011 orders for 1979 at 33.[7] All of this simply suggests that market conditions can change with little advance warning, completely upsetting the pattern of dominance in the industry.

Competition in the Aircraft Engine Sector

Dominance in the aircraft engine market is, if anything, even more pronounced than in airframes. The four-firm sales concentration ratio for aircraft engines and engine parts increased from 58 percent in 1963 to 74 percent in 1972. Even more dramatic is the fact that the ratio for complete military aircraft engines was 96 percent and for non-military engines, 92 percent[8] (see Table 4.3). In the large commercial transport market, virtually all turbine engines produced outside the Soviet bloc are manufactured by Pratt & Whitney, General Electric, and Rolls Royce, and within this group P&W accounted for almost three quarters of all orders between 1966 and 1978. It is for this reason that New England is considered the jet engine capital of the world.

The Commercial Jet Engine Market

Rivalry in the commercial airframe market is known to be extremely intense, for the first company to enter the market with a new generation of equipment usually captures a major portion of it. As a result the opening stakes are very high. Competition in the jet engine market is even keener, however, for in addition to this factor, the interchangeability of engines on newer model aircraft forces each engine producer to compete head-on for the business of airlines and military aircraft procurement agencies.

Table 4.3 **Four-Firm Sales Concentration Ratios, Aircraft Industry Divisions, 1963 and 1972**

1972 SIC Code	Division	Ratio 1963	Ratio 1972
3721	Aircraft	58	69
37211	Military Aircraft	68	74
37212	Personal and Utility Aircraft	85	74
37213	Commercial Aircraft	94	97
3724	Aircraft Engines and Parts	58	74
37241	Military Aircraft Engines	97	96
37242	Non-Military Aircraft Engines	—	92
37243	Aeronautical Services on Engines (R&D)	87	83
37244	Engine Parts and Accessories	53	57
37285	Aircraft Propellers	87	81

SOURCES: Bureau of the Census, U.S. Department of Commerce, *Census of Manufacturers*, 1972. U.S. Congress, Subcommittee on Antitrust and Monopoly, Committee on the Judiciary, U.S. Senate, *Concentration Ratios in Manufacturing Industry, 1963, 1966*, 89th Congress, Second Session.

This consideration is important in sales of both retrofit and original equipment.

With stringent EPA regulations on noise, fuel efficiency, and pollution, some airlines have decided to upgrade their planes with new engines. In the past, original equipment suppliers were almost assured of additional sales when spare engines were needed for normal replacement. Today, however, airlines often choose to re-equip their planes with engines produced by manufacturers other than the original suppliers. The decision by United Airlines to replace the P&W JT3D engines on their DC-8-61s with GE/SNECMA turbofans is a case in point. Under the terms of the agreement, United will purchase $400 million worth of engines from GE to retrofit 30 of its DC-8s.[9] Other airlines are considering similar moves, forcing Pratt & Whitney to reassess its position in this especially competitive sector of the market.

Similarly, the interchangeability of engines has become important in the market for original equipment sales. As a result of customer preferences in jet engine purchases, airframes are now built to accept any one of several turbine configurations. The Boeing 747, for example, is capable of being powered by engines built by all three turbojet manufacturers. Thus, these firms are increasingly geared toward marketing to airlines rather than airframe manufacturers, as has historically been the case. This situation puts the airlines in a more powerful position as they can force each engine manufacturer to make its own sales presentation and then weigh offers of various concessions and guarantees before making a final decision. This factor has added a new wrinkle to the "King of the Mountain" competition engaged in by the primes.

Pratt & Whitney and General Electric are still number one and two in the military and commercial markets, but until quite recently General Electric's Aircraft Engine Group (AEG) held an extremely distant second place overall. As late as 1966, it received only 1.7 percent of all orders for large commercial aircraft turbines while P&W received over 92 percent. By 1978, nearly 10 years after the introduction of wide-bodied aircraft with interchangeable engine configurations, GE had captured almost a quarter of the new order market while Pratt & Whitney's share dropped to 63 percent. The balance went to Rolls Royce and the SNECMA consortium (see Figure 4.1). Interchangeability of engines clearly played a key role in GE's re-emergence as a turbojet power.

The history of the earlier competition is worth noting. While Pratt & Whitney provided Boeing and Douglas with the successful JT-3, General Electric was virtually shut out of the commercial end of the industry from the early 1960s to 1968 as a result of massive losses suffered in equipping the Convair 880s and 990s. According to at least one industry expert, the Convair airplanes were well designed, but they still failed in the marketplace.[10]

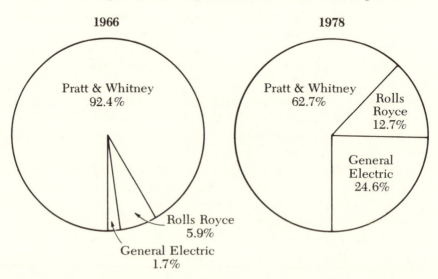

Figure 4.1 Share of Commercial Turbine Jet Engine Orders by Producer, 1966 and 1978. (*Source: Author's interviews with industry officials.*)

Like all of Boeing's competition, the Convairs arrived late on the market, a condition that was aggravated by contract provisions stipulated by TWA, its major purchaser. TWA persuaded Convair's builder, General Dynamics, to accept the condition that no 880s would be sold to anyone else for a year, a condition that was intended to assure supply. As it turned out it was demand and not supply that posed the problem.

With too few orders for the 880s, General Dynamics tried to recoup by adding new technology instead of cutting its losses. In 1958 it designed the 990, a full-scale jetliner, hoping to compete with the 707 and DC-8. The 990 did not sell in any quantity, with only 37 being built. Its timing was even worse than the 880s, coming out in 1961 during a period of overcapacity for the airlines. The 880/990 program was a financial albatross, losing a total of over $550 million for its builder, General Dynamics, and its engine designer, GE.

The Convair fiasco has been described as "the greatest American business failure in recorded history." The second greatest failure was the engine for it. When a firm commits extensive financial resources to the development and production of an engine, it expects to recoup its investment by equipping a large number of aircraft with it, as well as securing additional engine sales for replacement purposes. With the small production runs of the 880/990 program, however, GE could not even approach the break-even point on the engine program. *Forbes* magazine recently estimated GE's loss on the project to be approximately $150 million.[11] As customer service and product support are major components of any jet engine purchase, GE had to support the engines continually if it hoped to ever regain a foothold in the industry. As it was, GE did not ship another large commercial aircraft turbine from 1962 to 1966.

GE's AEG division was sustained in the jet engine market throughout the 1960s only by reason of its military production, and even here, in trying to exist solely as a government supplier, it was the victim of numerous economic reverses. The first involved the Air Force's C5A transport program for which GE received a $459 million contract as engine developer.[12] Since development contracts rarely cover all costs incurred, much of the development cost is amortized during the production run. By 1970, however, well-publicized design flaws in the airframe built by Lockheed caused the government to curtail C5A orders, and

GE took a substantial loss on the project. Following this loss, it appeared that GE's luck would improve, but again it ran into a string of misfortune, stemming from what initially appeared to be success. GE bid successfully on the development of its F101 engine for the SST program and then was successful again on the B-1 bomber project. According to a company spokesman at the time, "either of these projects could have put the company in the large commercial jet engine business up to its hips."[13] But no production contract materialized for the SST, and in 1971 Congress discontinued funding for the project altogether. GE's loss was over $50 million. Six years later, after GE had built engines for seven B-1 bomber prototypes at a price of well over $400 million, President Carter terminated production funding for the B-1, again taking away a potentially lucrative market from the GE division.

The terminations of the SST and B-1 bomber programs are illustrative of the political nature of "demand" conditions in the industry. The political process is the "wild card" in this competitive forum. The circumstances surrounding the discontinuance of the SST program merit special scrutiny in this regard. When Richard Nixon took office in January 1969, he was confronted with the decision of whether or not to continue work on the controversial supersonic transport. The main arguments of SST proponents were economic, that is, potential job creation, potential export market, and the need to maintain American aerospace preeminence. Opponents advanced ecological arguments, such as the possible destruction of the earth's ozone layer and excessive noise pollution. Some members of Congress had political reservations about public funding of the program given the widespread belief that such a project should be financed privately instead of through tax dollars. Given the experience of the French–English Concorde, however, it was clear that private capital would find such an undertaking financially too risky.

Funding of the program for fiscal year 1970 was barely appropriated after a congressional battle. Legislators and lobbyists marshalled their forces for the congressional struggle that was certain to take place during the next year's budget hearings. Senators Jackson and Magnuson of Washington were the chief pro-SST senators; aligned against them were Senator Proxmire of Wisconsin and the Friends of the Earth, a registered lobbyist for the ecology movement.

The pro-SST camp was composed of a coalition of prime contractors (Boeing and General Electric), labor unions, and organizations from various states in which SST development would be carried out. Some of their tactics were at once bitter and comic: Seattle (Boeing's home) considered a boycott of Wisconsin cheese, and in some state legislatures, resolutions were introduced that would have banned made-in-Wisconsin Evinrude motors from state waterways! Despite these and other more serious actions, and despite the depressed employment condition in the industry, funding of the SST was discontinued in May 1971.

The SST and C5A setbacks would have put GE out of the aircraft turbine industry altogether, except for the fact that the development contract for the B-1 plus GE's own internal financing provided the basis for producing the commercial CF6, an engine especially well suited for transports such as the DC-10, the L-1011 Tristar, and the European-built A300 Airbus. Prior to the introduction of these wide-bodied aircraft, virtually all commercial airliners built by Boeing and Douglas were powered by Pratt & Whitney engines. When the CF6 was introduced, however, Douglas chose to power its DC-10s with this engine. Moreover, because Boeing had increased the design weight of the 747 until it exceeded the original thrust requirements of P&W's JT9D engine (an engine that competes against the CF6), GE and Rolls Royce were able to place their engines on some of the 747s bound for the overseas market, an airline market that could not afford to wait for an improved JT9D.[14] GE was also the victor in the competition to provide engines for the A300 Airbus. This aircraft had been originally designed to utilize only Rolls Royce power; but when the Rolls engine fell behind schedule and Great Britain pulled out of the Airbus consortium altogether, the organization opted for the GE CF6-50, which had been developed for the DC-10. All of these factors allowed GE to challenge the almost absolute dominance of Pratt & Whitney in the commercial market.

Sales of the CF6 were strong enough to have two important effects upon GE's competitive standing. Primarily, it provided GE with the cash flow necessary to develop new derivative engines, including the clipped fan CF6-32 and the CF6-80, that are proposed as power plants for the new Boeing 757s and 767s as well as future versions of the Airbus transports. Second, it gave GE a strong marketing position in relation to the current re-equipment cycle for which these turbines are considered ideal. Engine commonality with other aircraft in a customer's fleet will play an important role in this cycle as opposed to cycles of the past, and it will likely benefit GE in its continuing challenge to Pratt & Whitney's dominance. British Caledonian Airways, to cite one instance, recently chose the CF6-80 to power the Airbus A310s it ordered, citing a 40-percent commonality factor with GE engines already operating in its DC-10s as a major factor in the decision.[15]

The CF6-32, the GE turbine that could power the 757, has achieved a substantial lead time over the new Pratt & Whitney JT10D, which the firm has been working on for several years, apparently for a time without a total commitment of financial resources from its parent company, United Technologies Corporation. It was not until late 1979, when UTC apparently recognized the competitive threat posed by GE, that corporate management announced its decision to spend $700 million to complete development of the engine. UTC stated that $300 million already had been spent since the mid-1970s for preliminary development work and that $700 million would be spent on the project over the next several years.[16] Scheduled for certification by aviation authorities sometime in 1984, the JT10D is being developed for the 757, as well as for other aircraft still in the design stage, such as contemplated stretched versions of the Boeing 727, a long-range version of the Airbus, which is currently on the drawing board, and McDonnell Douglas' proposed ATMR airliner.

The UTC announcement of a commitment of $1 billion to the JT10D brought no surprising response from GE's Aircraft Engine Group. Brian Rowe, senior vice president of the division, made it clear that "We aren't going to stand still. Obviously, we're going to protect our market share," including refining the CF6-32 to improve its fuel consumption to match the performance of the new Pratt & Whitney engine.[17] Indeed, P&W's decision to move ahead quickly with development of the engine has signaled a new era in which there will likely be even more intense competition between the three major engine manufacturers.

Since the JT10D is the only totally new jet engine being designed specifically for the new generation of medium-size jets, it may indeed have a major advantage over the offerings of competitors, especially in terms of fuel efficiency. Both GE and Rolls Royce have scaled down their larger wide-body engines to fit the new medium-range jets. Therefore, Pratt may be the only manufacturer that will be able to offer the latest state-of-the-art technology in its new engines. With customer demand for timely delivery such a critical factor in aircraft and engine sales, it is impossible to know whether the technology differential will be as great a marketing advantage as Pratt hopes it to be. Boeing executive Robert Purdue recently offered the following suggestion, however:[18]

> *Some airlines think that Pratt & Whitney is the only engine manufacturer there is, and they may wait. Since they (Pratt & Whitney) are building an all-new engine, they should be able to offer something extra. They are going to have to, if they come out two years late.*

The success of P&W in winning the competition to equip the newly ordered Delta and American airlines 757s with their JT10D appears to be strong testimony to Purdue's point.

The competition involved in persuading airlines to choose one aircraft engine rather than another obviously does not apply to Boeing aircraft alone. While all of the American carriers except Eastern were choosing the 767 in the ongoing re-equipment cycle, most European lines were opting for the Airbus Industrie A300 and A310 series. Throughout the 1970s General Electric was able to practically exclude Pratt & Whitney from the Airbus market by virtue of its initial success in providing the earliest A300s with its turbines. It was not unexpected, then, that Pratt & Whitney would make a zealous attempt to capture a larger share of this lucrative European market.

The most significant and widely publicized episode in the competition involved the hard-fought battle over an engine contract for Air France's five firm orders and ten options on the A310. Because Air France's choice was expected to exert strong influence on the engine selections of Mid Eastern and African airlines, the competition was considered especially critical.

Pratt & Whitney's determination to upstage GE was evident in the considerable financial incentives it offered in attempting to gain Air France as a customer. Included in Pratt & Whitney's financial package was an offer to refurbish the airline's aging JT9D engines, which power its 747s, at no cost to Air France—an offer estimated to be worth $35 million.[19] In addition, the engine manufacturer offered to assist the airline in building a maintenance facility for the Airbus engines in France, an attractive proposition because it would have minimized the amount of time that the carrier's planes would need to spend in the current maintenance base located in Hamburg, Germany.[20] Finally, Pratt & Whitney offered to subcontract to French industry a share of the production equal to 30 percent of the value of all A300/A310 engines sold. If a projected growth in sales were to be realized by Airbus, this offer could have amounted to over $1 billion worth of work to French aircraft firms over the next 15 years.[21]

An outside observer would obviously consider such an offer to be quite enticing to the French, but as it turned out other political factors won the day for GE. The management of Air France, as well as the French Transport Ministry, apparently favored the Pratt & Whitney offer. The Defense Ministry and various labor unions were staunchly opposed to the P&W deal, however. They cited the government's original $500 million investment in the GE/SNECMA joint venture, the future trade benefits to be derived from that relationship, and the jobs that it potentially encompassed as reasons to select the GE engine. This "coalition" succeeded in imposing its will upon both Air France and the Transport Ministry. The GE turbofans were ultimately chosen, but according to an Air France official, not without a GE offer that included "financial conditions equally as advantageous as those proposed by Pratt & Whitney."[22]

If this trend continues, Standard and Poor has suggested that "the present dominant market position enjoyed by Pratt & Whitney could fall to GE within 10 years."[23] The result would be a significant shift in the fortunes of the two firms. Pratt & Whitney can be expected to exert a tremendous effort to see that this does not occur. Its initial success in the 757 market suggests that it is fully prepared to take on the competition.

The Military Jet Engine Market

GE always fared much better within the military market than in the lucrative commercial sphere. It won over 50 percent of the Defense Department turbine contracts during the 1960s.[24] But as GE gained in the commercial sphere in the 1970s, Pratt & Whitney began to challenge it in the military sector. P&W's F100 jet engine now powers three of the major U.S. and NATO fighters, the F-14, F-15, and F-16. The contract for the F-16 is considered to be the plum of all recent military contracts because four of the NATO allies agreed to purchase this General Dynamics plane over its Swedish SAAB and French Dessault competitors, as well as over the Northrup/GE powered F-17. Plans call for the Air Force to purchase 1,388 aircraft at a total price of $13.8 billion. In addition, orders have been placed by NATO countries for another 348 planes. Including potential foreign sales, billings over a 15-year period could reach $20 billion for this one aircraft.

Here again, the political nature of demand for the industry's product deserves note. Throughout the mid and late 1970s Pratt & Whitney ran into trouble with its military products because of quality and performance problems. In May 1975 the Air Force grounded 20 F-15 fighters because of cracked turbine blades.[25] In June of the same year, the Navy grounded 600 F-14 fighters because of engine fan failure. Most serious of all was the fact that Pratt & Whitney's F-16 power plants were prone to total airborne failure.[26] In 1978 the General Accounting Office reported that "the rate of loss for the F-16 due to engine failure is currently estimated by the Air Force to be three times higher than that called for by Air Force specifications. . . . The F100 engine problems on the F-16 are serious because it has only one engine."[27] The problems became so severe that the firm was forced to redesign and modify parts of the turbine. The changes are being incorporated into all new F100s, and all existing power plants are to be modified as well. Yet this was only the beginning of Pratt & Whitney's troubles with its top military engine.

A second problem encountered by the company with the F100 involved late engine deliveries caused by work stoppages at two of its major vendors. In October 1979 Air Force officials predicted that the shortfall in engine deliveries to the armed services could be approximately 200 units by the end of 1980 but that the number was subject to change as productivity at Pratt & Whitney's vendors would be the crucial determinant of the speed of recovery.[28]

Winston Williams, writing in the *New York Times*, underscored the impact of these difficulties upon Pratt & Whitney's operations: "The F100 is Pratt's major government contract and its thin profit margins are expected to grow thinner as the company tries to correct the stalling problem and to catch up on deliveries."[29] But thinner profit margins may be the least of Pratt & Whitney's problems. The Air Force and Navy were sufficiently concerned with Pratt's difficulties to provide funding for a three-year development program in which General Electric is to develop an alternative turbine, the F101 derivative fighter engine (DFE), capable of powering the F-15 and F-16. Since this program is currently receiving only limited financial support from the Defense

Department, its impact on Pratt & Whitney's competitive position in the military market is merely a matter for conjecture. If and when the Defense Department decides to make a full-scale commitment to GE's derivative, however, Pratt undoubtedly will be faced with the same type of challenge it was confronted with in the commercial sphere.

The firm has, in fact, already implemented a previously unheard-of policy in the military fighter jet engine market that must be construed as a reaction to increasing competition in this market segment. In May 1980 it was reported that Pratt & Whitney was offering a new F100 turbine warranty to the Air Force to begin with engines delivered in early 1981. The warranty will cover any turbine failure caused by deterioration or structural failure that occurs within two years of F-15 or F-16 service. Repairs and replacements will be made by the manufacturer at no increase in the production contract price. Such a liberal guarantee has never been offered before.

What is even more revealing about the nature of the new competition is that within one month of Pratt & Whitney's announcement of an F100 warranty, General Electric responded with its own offer of a turbine warranty for the F101 DFE. GE's version will cover any turbine failure caused by wearout or structural failure that occurs within *four* years of new fighter service, or twice the coverage offered by Pratt & Whitney. Clearly, the intensity of competition has reached the point where specific marketing strategies are being matched one for one by the two concerns. In this case, General Electric was quite obviously unwilling to let Pratt & Whitney implement a policy that would have given it a significant competitive edge in this market segment. The military jet engine battle may therefore just be warming up.

Other Segments of the Engine Market: General Aircraft and Helicopter Sales

Also affecting the turbine market is a shift in the complexion of the business aircraft and helicopter markets. There are more competitors in the general aircraft segment than in any other part of the market, and the rivalry is just as intense. Technological advances made in the development of more sophisticated airplanes are filtering down to general business aircraft and helicopters, which may now be ordered with advanced avionic equipment, turbofan engines, or turboprop propulsion units.

Garrett AiResearch, Pratt & Whitney, and General Electric dominate the manufacture of turbines for small, fixed-wing jets. Detroit Diesel-Allison, Avco Lycoming, and General Electric dominate the manufacture of helicopter turbines. Until recently, General Electric had 50 percent of the total business jet engine market, but Garrett and Pratt & Whitney have eroded GE's position.[30] General Electric's engines have been losing ground in the marketplace to these two firms because of the newer and more fuel-efficient engines designed by these companies specifically for the civilian engine market. GE has chosen to offer only turbines that are derivatives of its small military power plants, and therefore the company is finding it difficult to compete effectively with its competitors' new products. Pratt & Whitney, which reported having 28 percent of the business jet engine market in 1977, obviously expects this trend to continue, for P&W forecasts an increase of its market share to 43 percent over the 10-year period ending in 1987.[31]

Nevertheless, in the helicopter turbine market General Electric appears to have few worries from its competitors. The company recently (1978) won a contract to manufacture T700 engines for the Army Black Hawk helicopter. Each Black Hawk will be powered by two T700s, and 1,100 of the craft are to be procured. In addition, this turbine is to be used in two other military helicopters and also in several civilian applications (the commercial version of the engine is called the CT7). Including sales to foreign countries, GE expects the total demand to reach 15,000 units.[32] The T700s are being assembled in Lynn, Massachusetts, with components being made in Lynn and other AEG plants in Rutland, Vermont, and Hooksett, New Hampshire. The Army estimates that the contract will provide employment for up to 900 AEG employees a year and will create an additional 400 to 600 jobs within GE's subcontractor network.[33]

The Helicopter Market

The commercial market for aircraft goes back to at least the 1930s and the military market to World War I. But it was not until the Korean War that the newest form of manned aircraft, the helicopter, became recognized as a highly useful weapon with unique military capabilities. The Sikorsky helicopters built during World War II were in service by 1944, but because of the late hour of the war, they were not given the opportunity to display their operational capabilities fully. During the Korean War, however, helicopters were found to be extraordinarily useful in evacuating wounded soldiers from combat areas and in transporting troops and supplies into and out of areas that had been previously thought of as inaccessible. MASH units were dependent on them. This recognition was reflected in the dramatic rise in helicopter sales between 1946 and 1952; the sale of military units rose from 44 in 1946 to 983 in 1952, the peak year of the war.[34]

Immediately following the Korean conflict, there was a sharp reduction in military helicopter procurement. Military production fell from 943 units in 1953 to 431 a year later, a decline of 54 percent.[35] Since there was virtually no commercial market at the time (131 helicopters were produced for non-military use in 1954),[36] manufacturers were unable to offset the drastic military decline. Analogous to other segments of the aircraft industry, the helicopter sector displayed an equal susceptibility to the boom-or-bust nature of defense spending.

Historically, government-sponsored outlays for research and development have been far smaller in the helicopter sector than in the conventional aircraft or missile sectors of the industry. This distinction was especially true during the 1950s when the Defense Department began to make massive financial commitments to missile development, diverting large amounts of potential R&D funding away from the helicopter in the process. As a result, only three large military competitions were initiated during the decade.[37] The first, announced in 1954 by the Army, was won the following year by Bell Helicopter with its UH-1 "Huey," which subsequently became the ubiquitous helicopter in Viet-Nam. Because no other military contracts were available at that time to help underwrite R&D costs, Bell's competitors did not attempt to build an aircraft to compete with the Huey. This decision, dictated by financial necessity, effectively insured Bell's hold on a major part of the military market throughout the Viet-Nam era.

The second large competition of the decade was initiated in 1958 when the Army decided to replace its piston-powered transports with larger and faster turbine engine helicopters. Vertol, a Philadelphia-based manufacturer, won this competition in 1959 with its enormous Chinook transport, effectively securing the second major portion of the military business for years to come. Finally, in late 1959 a Defense Department committee met to consider the Army's requirements for the upcoming decade. A decision to standardize the Huey and Chinook was made, as well as a decision to initiate a competition to provide the Army with an entirely new light observation craft. After design proposals were submitted and reviewed, the competition was narrowed to three manufacturers—Bell, Hughes, and Hiller—who were awarded prototype development funding. In 1964 Hughes emerged as the winner of the competition, and the third and final major portion of the Army helicopter market had been secured.

Although it is generally assumed that the Viet-Nam War greatly enhanced Sikorsky's position as a manufacturer in the military market, the preceding history indicates that this was not the case. The firm was not particularly successful in selling its products to the military. In fact, in 1966 80 percent of all U.S. military purchases of helicopters were from Bell and Vertol.[38] According to the April 1966 issue of *Fortune* magazine, Sikorsky's plant in Stratford, Connecticut, was operating at only 40 percent of capacity at the time.[39]

The company was, however, one of the few manufacturers in the industry to build new helicopters without the aid of military research and development contracts. For example, the firm used its own funds to develop the Flying Crane, a large cargo transport for which development costs approached $10 million.[40]

While Bell and Vertol continued to produce their older design aircraft, Sikorsky used funds from its parent company, United Technologies, in combination with government R&D funds to develop an entirely new helicopter transport. Their R&D efforts paid off in 1977 when the company displaced Bell and Vertol as the leaders in helicopter contracting after the Army chose Sikorsky's Utility Tactical Transport Aircraft System (UTTAS) over Vertol's version. The Army initiated the competitive development program for this aircraft in 1972 in order to obtain a technologically sophisticated and effective attack helicopter to replace the aging Bell UH-1 "Huey." The aircraft to emerge as the winner of that competition was the Sikorsky UTTAS, more commonly known as the Black Hawk. The final choice of Sikorsky's design over the Vertol version was a result of what the *Journal of Commerce* called "better performance and production readiness."[41]

The ultimate value of the UTTAS contract, which requires that

1,100 troop transport helicopters be delivered by 1985, has been estimated at $3.4 billion, and it means approximately 2,000 new jobs in Sikorsky's Stratford, Connecticut, plant over the life of the eight-year contract.[42] In addition to the UTTAS contract, in 1978 Sikorsky won the competition to develop the Light Airborne Multi-Purpose System (LAMPS) for the Navy. LAMPS will be similar to the Army's Black Hawk, but will be modified to Navy specifications. A production decision estimated to be worth about $700 million is expected sometime in 1981. In the military sector Sikorsky is also producing the CH-53E Super Stallion, a heavy transport helicopter. The total program for the Navy may amount to 100 units valued at more than $750 million.

In addition to experiencing substantial growth in the defense sector, the helicopter industry has undergone an explosion in commercial sales. The civilian segment, as a proportion of the total helicopter market, has grown dramatically over the past 15 years. In 1975 the Sikorsky division, for example, claimed that its military/commercial sales mix had moved from a high of 90/10 during the 1960s to a more balanced 50/50.[43] This significant turn-around undoubtedly provided some degree of insulation, at least for a time, against the government-induced volatility to which the helicopter segment has been especially susceptible.

Because of recent economic and performance gains, particularly with respect to maintenance, commercial helicopters are now being employed in a full range of applications. Today helicopters operate at speeds and ranges far in excess of those available just 10 years ago. Broad new markets in both executive transportation and commuter air travel are opening up for the first time to helicopter manufacturers as a result of the machine's greatly increased capabilities. Industry sources maintain that the new generation of helicopters will be competitive with turboprop and turbofan fixed-wing business jets on 300- to 400-mile missions, thereby making corporate and executive transportation a potentially lucrative field. Moreover, a new airline commuter market, generated by airline deregulation, has been cited as a potentially significant factor for manufacturers.

As in the military sphere, Sikorsky has been especially successful in capturing a substantial share of this rapidly growing commercial market. The UTC division is, at this writing, fully booked for the production of its S-76 aircraft, a model that marks the first time a commercial helicopter was designed from the ground up specifically for non-military use. In the past, commercial models have been exclusively derivatives of military versions. Reports in 1980 indicated that Sikorsky's backlog for the S-76 exceeded 325 units and extended well into 1983, with 124 new sales in 1979 alone.[44]

All of this is clear evidence that the world helicopter market is booming, with Sikorsky taking the leading share. Yet new long-term modernization programs, sponsored by the military, are expected to benefit the companies that lost in the UTTAS and LAMPS competitions, specifically Bell and Vertol. Under these modernization programs (dubbed CILOP—Conversion in Lieu of Procurement), conversion to advanced helicopters by incorporating new technology into existing airframes and flight systems will permit the extension of the life of the current military helicopter fleet well into the 1990s. It is expected that CILOP programs will help to maintain a strong U.S. helicopter manufacturing base, as well as provide a significant market for vendors supplying retrofit equipment. This planned upgrading of existing helicopters in both foreign and domestic military fleets is expected to keep the sales of Sikorsky's rivals at a profitable level well into the 1980s. This perhaps provides another indication of the political nature of the aircraft market. Price, quality, on-time delivery, and maintainability all play a role in determining which firms dominate the market, but the part that politics plays cannot be overlooked.

Competition in the Subcontractor Market

Up to this point the focus of the discussion on market competition has been on the prime contractor. The other half of the aircraft industry, the critical constellation of job shops and suppliers that subcontract to the chief airframe and engine producers, has been largely ignored. It is to an analysis of this segment that we now turn.

The structure of the subcontractor market bears little resemblance to the market-dominant form of the primes. Although some of the subcontractors are themselves Fortune 500 firms, the majority consist of small companies with 250 or fewer employees. These firms bear the brunt of competition in the industry.

In 1968 there were over 6,000 major aerospace subcontractors in the United States and abroad. The large drop in industry sales in 1968–1971, in concert with increases in the make/buy ratios of the primes, devastated the subcontractor network. Circumstances surrounding the near bankruptcy of Lockheed provide a particularly vivid illustration of this phenomenon. To avoid shutting down altogether, Lockheed brought much of its vendor business inside in fiscal 1970. In so doing the company canceled contracts with over 1,800 individual suppliers. By late 1977, it is estimated that only 3,700 of the original 6,000 subcontractors operating in 1968 were still in business.[45] The rest either went bankrupt or sought business elsewhere. One reason for the large number of business failures is that as work becomes scarce, the subs find it increasingly difficult to underbid their competitors and still cover variable costs. In addition, in periods of severe inflation subcontracts at fixed prices can result in huge, unanticipated losses.

Subcontracting is risky even in relatively stable times. If a supplier has a disagreement with the prime contractor over pricing or performance, the prime can simply drop the vendor and go to another supplier. Prime contractors, on the other hand, are often in a sheltered position; if they encounter developmental problems, the government is often under pressure to accept the added cost of the solution or face the loss of a particular defense system if it elects termination. A number of subcontractors in New England were nearly forced into bankruptcy when the Lockheed C5A contracts were curtailed, whereas the prime contractor was bailed out with its famous government loan guarantee of $250 million. One dismayed vendor who was a victim of the Lockheed episode told us that he was frustrated by the fact that "Lockheed got big help from the government, but our little company got nothing. There is no law to protect us little guys from them."

Through at least the early 1960s, subcontractor constellations located in close geographic proximity to the primes provided a large number of aircraft components. Single vendors were responsible for individual parts, and a largely symbiotic relationship prevailed between suppliers and the primes. Since that time the subcontractor network has been geographically dispersed, and the primes have so positioned themselves as to have multiple sources for many of the components they purchase. This is usually not because a single supplier is too small to produce the full complement of parts, but because the primes do not wish to remain dependent on single sources. Although the case of the F100 engines has already been mentioned, it merits additional comment here.

In spring 1979, strikes at two major suppliers caused production bottlenecks at both GE and Pratt & Whitney. Workers at Ladish Company, a major forging manufacturer, and Fafnir Bearing Company, a principal producer of precision bearings and a division of Textron, went on strike at virtually the same time, forcing Pratt & Whitney to seek alternative suppliers. It accelerated its purchases from other subcontractors to reduce the impact of the two strikes, but nonetheless, the company fell far behind in deliveries of its military F100 engines as well as some of its commercial JT9Ds. In referring to the strike at Ladish, Harry Gray, the chairman of UTC, remarked,[46]

We have got a work-around program there. Just recently, we picked up 25 tons of material and flew it to another supplier, and we got the other supplier working. We are going to do everything possible to support both our military and our commercial customers so that it will minimize the impact of the strike.

Since supply shortages also stem from a scarce supply of skilled labor, primes have begun to select second sources that are geographically dispersed, a strategy made possible by declining transportation and communication costs. With the advent of the new generation of commercial aircraft, a much larger number of foreign firms have entered the subcontracting field. Exemplifying this trend, Boeing has contracted with a consortium of Japanese companies for 15 percent of the work on the 767, while the Italian government's Aeritalia will perform an additional 15 percent.

Interviews with New England subcontractors confirmed the apparent growth in multiple vendor arrangements and foreign sourcing as leading causes of increased competition in the industry. Several subcontractors felt that their fate was outside their control, and there were numerous complaints that second-source contracts were given to competitors even when the original vendor's price was lower and the quality of its parts superior. One of the largest small parts vendors in Connecticut argued that it was eminently competitive with other machine shops in the area and on the West Coast and could easily supply the primes with all of the parts they needed. In recent years, however, at least one prime contractor has refused to grant the vendor sole-source status. In the two years following the peak of Viet-Nam production, employment at this vendor declined from 1,800 to 500. A smaller job shop employing 255 workers, which until recently was the sole supplier of turbine rings for another prime contractor, must now share its market with an English firm under an arrangement negotiated between the prime and the United Kingdom. A still smaller sub-contractor lists 10 competitors in New York, 2 in Maine, and 2 in Connecticut.

Despite the dispersal of the vendor market, prime contractors themselves remain the chief competitors to the subs. By varying the make/buy ratio over the market cycle and always maintaining the threat to bring production inside if the vendor fails to meet price or quality standards, the primes have further boosted competition in the supplier market. The surviving vendor appears to be the firm with the capability of performing manifold operations and manufacturing complete parts that other firms cannot. Several interviewed in New England mentioned they have survived only because they have developed special tools, jigs, or processes in-house that made them unique in their end of the industry.

The effect of subcontractor dispersal and multiple sourcing has not only been heightened competition, but also ultimately a substantial failure rate among many well-established local vendors. An analysis of the aircraft firms listed in *Hall's New England Directory of Manufacturers* shows that nearly half of the existing subcontractors in 1959 were gone by 1978. Presumably most of them went out of business, while some may have been absorbed into larger firms. Another substantial portion continued in business, but they were no longer listed as producing for the aircraft and parts industry.

The fate of the small and medium-size subcontractor is further illustrated by Dun & Bradstreet establishment data for New England.[47] Table 4.4 indicates that during the period of sharp decline (1969–1972), establishments with 50 or fewer employees suffered the highest mortality rate: 27 percent or 24 of the 90 firms in the Dun & Bradstreet sample went out of business during this shake-out period. In terms of employment, firms with 500 employees or less accounted for just 17.5 percent of total SIC 372 employment in 1969, but over 65 percent of all net job loss during the ensuing three-year period. The large prime contractors, meanwhile, experienced only a 4.5 percent decline in their employment as they increased their make/buy ratios and canceled subcontractor agreements.

During the slow growth period of 1972–1974, establishment births in the region occurred only among the smallest firms, and the greatest employment growth appeared within the vendor constellation (see Table 4.5). With only 15.7 percent of total em-

Table 4.4 **Components of Establishment and Employment Change, 1969–1972, Aircraft and Parts—All New England**

	Establishments			
Size	*1969 Total*	*Net Change*	*Birth*	*Death*
0–50	90	− 18.9%	7.8%	− 26.7%
51–500	52	− 15.4	1.9	− 17.3
501 +	13	0	7.7	− 7.7
Total	155	− 16.9%	5.8%	− 21.9%

	Employment			
Size	*1969 Total*	*Net Change*	*Birth and Expansion*	*Death and Contraction*
0–50	1,677	− 27.4%	12.7%	− 40.1%
51–500	8,264	− 42.7	5.4	− 48.1
501 +	46,970	− 4.5	3.2	− 7.7
Total	56,911	− 10.7%	3.9%	− 14.6%

SOURCE: Special tabulations on Dun & Bradstreet establishment data, made available by David Birch, Laboratory for Neighborhood and Regional Change, MIT, May 1979.

Table 4.5 **Components of Establishment and Employment Change 1972–1974, Aircraft and Parts—All New England**

	Establishments			
Size	*1972 Total*	*Net Change*	*Birth*	*Death*
0–50	86	− 1.1%	11.6%	− 12.8%
51–500	43	0	0	0
501 +	12	0	0	0
Total	141	− 0.7%	7.1%	− 7.8%

	Employment			
Size	*1972 Total*	*Net Change*	*Birth and Expansion*	*Death and Contraction*
0–50	1,497	11.2%	25.7%	− 14.6%
51–500	5,564	13.3	17.6	− 4.3
501 +	37,900	2.4	2.4	0
Total	44,961	4.0%	5.0%	− 1.0%

SOURCE: Special tabulations on Dun & Bradstreet establishment data, made available by David Birch, Laboratory for Neighborhood and Regional Change, MIT, May 1979.

Table 4.6   **Components of Establishment and Employment Change
1974–1976, Aircraft and Parts—All New England**

	Establishments			
Size	*1974 Total*	*Net Change*	*Birth*	*Death*
0–50	82	− 8.5%	8.5%	−17.1%
51–500	45	2.2	4.4	− 2.2
501 +	11	−9.1	0	− 9.1
Total	138	−5.1%	6.5%	−11.6%

	Employment			
Size	*1974 Total*	*Net Change*	*Birth and Expansion*	*Death and Contraction*
0–50	1,366	7.2%	21.1%	−14.0%
51–500	6,329	4.4	10.8	− 6.4
501 +	25,460	−13.4	0.8	−14.2
Total	33,155	− 9.1%	3.5%	−12.6%

SOURCE: Special tabulations on Dun & Bradstreet establishment data, made available by David Birch, Laboratory for Neighborhood and Regional Change, MIT, May 1979.

ployment, these firms accounted for over half of all net employment growth, suggesting a pro-cyclical reduction in the make/buy ratio. The period of 1974–1976 would have been similar to the preceding brief era except for the failure of one of the large industry establishments, which was responsible for a displacement of approximately 1,600 workers (see Table 4.6).

With the geographical extension of multiple sourcing, normal cyclical volatility may now lead to even more adverse consequences for the regional subcontractor network. An asymmetrical relationship appears to be evolving in which the primes may further increase their make/buy ratios during downturns at the expense of local vendors. During subsequent upturns, the primes may seek to expand the vendor network and therefore not increase their demand for parts from their traditional constellation of vendors. The implications for regional employment are not heartening. The end result may be more stable employment, but with a much lower average employment level in the regional subcontractor network on both the East and West coasts.

New Competitive Factors in the Aircraft Industry

From the information presented so far, it is obvious that intense competition exists among subcontractors and that it is becoming more rampant as a result of the multiple-sourcing stratagem. Moreover, because of such factors as foreign competition, the battle among prime contractors may be turning into a case of an oligopolistic market in which historical dominance has begun to disintegrate. This situation is true in the aircraft turbine industry in New England, but it has also affected the airframe market throughout the country.

What is less understood is the nature of this competition, or stated differently, what aircraft producers offer to secure sales. Our research, and particularly our interviews with industry executives, suggests that the nature of competition in the prime market differs significantly from that in the vendor network. Among the large contractors, price plays a decidedly secondary role with quality, reliability, and especially on-time delivery being the key to market success.

In this light, one industry executive explained that his firm was able to market its $625,000 engine successfully against a competitor's similar turbine selling for $100,000 less by convincing potential buyers of his company's superior product support. He told us that he stressed one factor above all others to customers: ". . . you don't buy an engine—you buy an obligation; the purchase price is incidental." Other industry officials concurred with this assessment, particularly in regard to the commercial market. Post-sale support as a key determinant in procurement is more important than ever before because of the marketing strategy that forces jet engine producers to sell directly to airlines rather than airframe manufacturers. Air carriers are particularly concerned with ease of service, product reliability, parts availability, and the long-run minimization of operating costs.

Yet the real key to the domestic commercial market is still lead time and on-time manufacturing performance. According to an industry source, 70 percent of the market for a new aircraft entry is exhausted in 18 months. Late entrants to the market—such as Douglas' DC-8 and Lockheed's L-1011—are severely disadvantaged in their ability to market enough units to cover development costs. The early introduction of the CF6 turbine, which powers the DC-10 and other aircraft, allowed GE to capture 45 percent of the available market. Even then, industry sources indicate that the $865 million project cost will not be recouped before 1984.

The recent explosion in fuel costs and the growing incidence of spot shortages have provided the airlines with an added incentive to purchase new generation aircraft from manufacturers who can provide earliest delivery with the strongest assurance that there will be no delay in contract performance. This factor, in turn, has affected the production management decisions of the large turbine manufacturers. No airline wants to purchase an airframe built in Seattle, Washington, or Long Beach, California, only to have it sit on the runway apron awaiting engines to power it. Thus the engine producer, as well as the airframe manufacturer, has to convince potential customers of its ability to deliver on time.

It is this requirement that explains in large measure the motivation behind multiple sourcing and other strategies designed to minimize production disruptions. On-time contract performance requires prompt completion of the development and testing phase followed by a production run free of parts shortages and work stoppages. In the early stages, firms attempt to minimize development lead time by expending massive resources for R&D, by procuring Defense Department funds for the same purpose, and by entering into joint venture agreements in which they share capital costs and technology.

In the actual manufacturing stage, companies are relying on new production strategies. A move toward parallel production—duplicate facilities *within* the prime contractor's own production system—is apparently being made for reasons similar to those behind the multiple-sourcing strategy. Here the main concern is focused upon production disruptions that may occur as the result of work stoppages within their own organizations. The best examples are found among the engine producers. While the subcontractor workforce is generally not organized, both Pratt & Whitney and General Electric have had relatively militant union organizations, despite the inability of either major union, the International Union of Electrical Workers (IUE) or the International Association of Machinists (IAM), to secure union shop clauses at the two facilities. Late in the 1950s, GE led the march toward parallel production by establishing the non-union Ludlow, Vermont, plant. Then in the 1970s, it expanded its manufacturing holdings in Vermont by establishing another plant in Rutland. Its plan to spend $3 million for expansion of this facility in addition to a recently announced decision to set up an AEG facility to manufacture turbine blades and vanes in the non-unionized area of Madisonville, Kentucky, provides evidence that this strategy has grown increasingly popular with GE.

Pratt & Whitney has followed the same strategy for small turbine production by placing duplicate capacity in Canada and West Virginia. Pratt & Whitney's more recent move to North Berwick, Maine, provides the firm with non-union, backup capacity to its unionized North Haven, Connecticut, plant. Both facilities manufacture rotor blades and vanes. Parallel production of this type serves two purposes. It provides production capacity during company/union labor disputes, and it severely weakens the union's ability to strike in the first place. Multiple sourcing and parallel production strategies are now being adopted by other industries as well, in many cases taking their cue from the aircraft industry. Organized labor is justifiably anxious over such tactics, calling these moves part of the "new class warfare" against the worker.

Competition in the Military Market

New competitive strategies are by no means restricted to the commercial market. In the domestic military market, the Defense Department has been developing more cost-conscious procurement methods in the face of congressional reaction to cost overruns and until recently the declining share of the federal budget for defense. The new methods stress "design to unit production cost" and "design to life-cycle cost." These concepts have been formulated so that cost efficiency has become the most important procurement parameter. Furthermore, the Defense Department is placing more emphasis on reduced maintenance costs during the life cycle of each weapon, which has led to the new "RAM" strategy—*r*eliability, *a*vailability, and *m*aintainability. As a consequence, programs failing to meet these standards in the R&D stage will not proceed to production. This two-pronged procurement plan, cost plus RAM, has further increased competitive pressure.

Other changes in government procurement procedures, however, have increased defense contractor profit margins. In the "milestone" approach, the defense contractor is required to meet specific price and performance criteria at various "tilt points" throughout the life of the contract. To ease the problem of technology-related cost increases, there is widespread use of cost-plus contracts in the initial development phase. When the high-risk development stage is completed, straight fixed-price contracting is used in actual production. After this stage, if cost ceilings are exceeded or performance criteria are not met, the contractor faces possible termination of the program. By terminating an unprofitable program at an early stage, the contractor avoids consistent losses over a period of time.

Other changes in procurement methods include a return to the earlier concept of prototyping, or the practice of "fly before buy." Under this strategy, contractors build a number of prototypes, later testing them in competition with one another. The winner is selected on the basis of performance and production readiness for the manufacturing phase.

The New International Competition

In the international market, an entirely new vocabulary is needed to describe the competitive mechanisms used to sell aircraft. Concessions on co-production agreements, joint licensing arrangements, and offset requirements are often more important than price, and some have even inferred that they are more important than quality and maintainability. The key factor appears to be the degree to which a prime contractor is willing to share technology and employment gains with the purchaser nation. The sale of F-16s to the NATO alliance and F-15s to Japan are cases in point. In the NATO deal, General Dynamics and Pratt & Whitney promised that industries in the European countries ordering the plane would be allowed to produce 40 percent of the value of the 348 F-16s they were purchasing, 10 percent of the value of the 650 planes to be procured by the U.S. Air Force, and 15 percent of the value of those sold to other nations.[48] Industry sources maintain that NATO absolutely insisted on this co-production agreement as a requirement of placing orders for the U.S. fighter.

The sale of 100 F-15 fighters to the Japanese Self-Defense Force illustrates both the co-production phenomenon and the operation of international licensing arrangements. Of the 100 planes, 14 will be exported complete, 8 will be delivered in kit form to be assembled, and the remaining 78 will be produced in Japan by Mitsubishi and Kawasaki. Forty percent of the parts for the F-15 airframes will be imported from the United States as a result of the Air Force's reluctance to release high-technology classified components. Ishikawajima-Harima is being licensed by Pratt & Whitney to manufacture the 205 F100 engines for the 78 planes being produced abroad. The licensing agreement allows Pratt &

Whitney to reap a return on its R&D investment in the F100 without having to expand its production facilities or hire additional labor in the United States.

Offset agreements are also being used as "sweeteners," as one industry source put it, in order to secure international contracts. Under such an agreement, an exporter agrees to procure domestic markets for products of the purchaser nation. These agreements are now an inescapable competitive fact of life for virtually all aircraft producers. According to Robert Paul, director of material for Lockheed's California division, the firm has assigned two full-time people to survey the needs of other countries and to line up offset arrangements.[49] In still another instance, Northrup was able to sell F-5s powered by General Electric to the Swiss government by agreeing to aid in the sale of Swiss-made goods in the United States. It was rumored that the offset was 140 percent of the price of the aircraft and engine shipment. Part of the offset was in the form of purchased vendor supplies and raw materials for the F-5 itself.

One of the best-known examples involves the offset agreement instrumental in the F-16 NATO sale. Belgium was the last holdout in the agreement, the only one of the four NATO countries negotiating as a coalition undecided as to the relative merits of the F-16. When the U.S. government recognized that Belgium was delaying the sale, it agreed to purchase $30 million worth of machine guns from the Belgian arms firm, Fabrique Nationale. The deal pleased both parties. General Dynamics and Pratt & Whitney secured the sales they desperately wanted and Belgium obtained the jobs it said it needed. The desirability of such foreign military sales, even though they involve special agreements, comes from the fact that profit margins on foreign weapon shipments are said to be roughly twice as large as those on deliveries to the U.S. government.

The foreign demand for co-production and offset agreements became much more pronounced during the 1970s after many European manufacturers were given public subsidies or were nationalized. European private enterprise was simply unable to compete with American firms, but their governments were unwilling to sacrifice the export revenue or the jobs. In this context, the Airbus consortium was developed explicitly to distribute the heavy investment burden and the attendant risk among several firms, thereby reducing their competitive disadvantage. Once developed, these public and quasi-public enterprises used their new political clout to secure co-production and offset concessions.

To date, European industry has not seriously eroded American manufacturers' gross sales, but this is not necessarily indicative of the future. Within the past decade, for example, America's share of world aircraft exports has declined from 66 to 58 percent.[50] The Europeans hold a superior position to the Americans in two areas: finance and marketing. American firms are forced to compete with less risky borrowers in the traditional money markets, while the European consortia have the backing of several governments. In response, American firms have imitated their European competition by entering joint development ventures in order to garner investment capital. Firms such as Boeing, United Technologies, General Dynamics, and General Electric have adopted an "if you can't beat them—join them" strategy and formed various consortia with European firms. The partners involved in some of these agreements have been surprising at times. Ironically, SNECMA, the nationalized French concern that has produced General Electric engines under license, is owned in part by GE's arch rival, Pratt & Whitney; British Aerospace, another nationalized firm, is heavily involved with the development of two directly competing transports, the A310 and the Boeing 757.

These types of agreements are reported to be highly beneficial to all parties involved, for they allow European firms to gain the jobs necessary to keep their plants in operation, to gain American experience and technological know-how, and to diminish their competitive disadvantage. The benefits enjoyed by the American firms, meanwhile, lie in the securing of development capital (under the auspices of joint ventures) and the ability to make a highly profitable sale to a foreign country. As well as being beneficial to firms suffering from severe capital constraints, joint ventures provide the additional advantage of allowing American manufacturers to broaden their market base more effectively.

The impact of these agreements on U.S. aircraft workers is much more in dispute. Clearly, if more of the value of the Pratt & Whitney F100 military jet turbine or the GE/SNECMA CFM56 were built in the United States, there would be more jobs for American workers. Industry sources maintain, however, that without these international capital and production agreements, the foreign sales would not materialize at all and domestic employment would actually fall. Whether this is true or not depends on whether indigenous European products are indeed competitive with the advanced U.S. designs. Before the A300, they obviously were not. But the new European consortia are clearly becoming staunch competitors, partly as a result of the agreements themselves. By the end of 1979, in fact, worldwide orders for the Airbus were running significantly ahead of the wide-body sales of Boeing, Douglas, and Lockheed.

The narrowing of the technology gap between U.S. and foreign industries will likely lead to an even greater buildup of competition in world markets as it has in the auto industry and electronics. Jack Baranson, a technology expert, notes that the technology sold or shared in new international agreements is[51]

> . . . *increasingly the most sophisticated and recent generation available, and its release is often under terms that assure a rapid and efficient implantation of an internationally competitive productive capability. The trend represents a radical departure from the traditional transfer modes of direct foreign investment and licensing, in which the technology released was generally based on "mature" product lines and generally available production techniques.*

According to Baranson, corporate officials indicate concern that their corporate interests in selling state-of-the-art technology may not be in the best interests of the U.S. economy, but short-run profit imperatives demand these concessions.

Adding to the Foreign Challenge

According to a recent technology assessment by the Air Force, American manufacturing leadership is already being threatened by a new wave of foreign plant modernization that is designed to increase productivity and greatly lower the cost of the product.[52] Moreover, the study concludes that to be competitive, the United States must regain its momentum in the development of innovative manufacturing techniques. The European firms, aided by research at European institutes and universities, are rapidly introducing computer-aided manufacturing, and therefore they are approaching a time when they may hold a competitive edge over American firms in the production process. Then the issue will be whether U.S. firms can maintain the share of the European market that they now hold. In this case, depending to some extent upon the success of Airbus Industrie during the current airline re-equipment cycle, the American airframe industry may become less dominant in the world commercial transport market. With the entrance of the Joint European Transport Company (JET), a relatively new consortium of West European firms aiming to develop 100- to 200-seat aircraft, this trend may become more evident.

One growing factor in all of the foreign competition is the proliferation of European financial consortia willing to contribute large sums to finance the partial purchase of foreign aircraft by U.S. airlines. This is apparently true for the British BAC-111 and the European A300. These foreign banking consortia have arisen in response to American export market success bolstered by the U.S. Export-Import Bank. Standard & Poor reported in 1977 that:[53]

> *Over the past 10 years, Eximbank has provided $5.77 billion in loans covering the export sales of 1,185 commercial jets worth $12.8 billion. The lower effective rate of interest made possible by the participation of Eximbank, plus the extended period of repayment allowed by the bank, has proven to be very important to buyers that must plan on covering all repayment costs with operating earnings over the years.*

The Europeans have learned their lesson well and are now imitating it with success.

Within the helicopter market, there may be cause for even greater long-run concern over the competitive position of American manufacturers relative to European firms. Helicopters represent one of the few aircraft segments in which foreign manufacturers have long been competitive in the United States. Augusta of Italy, Aerospatiale of France, and Messerschmitt-Boelkow-Blohm (MBB) of West Germany are firmly established in the U.S. market, and they are increasing their presence and sales here each year, despite Sikorsky's recent successes.

Aerospatiale has been so successful in the U.S. market that it has established a wholly owned U.S. subsidiary, Aerospatiale Helicopter Corporation (AHC), in Texas. From its facility on the outskirts of Dallas, AHC expects to deliver 180 French-built helicopters in 1980, almost double the number it delivered in 1979.[54] By 1985 the firm expects to deliver approximately 300 aircraft annually.

Messerschmitt-Boelkow-Blohm also has recently begun to expand its presence in the United States. It recently established a wholly owned U.S. subsidiary, MBB Helicopter Corporation, in

West Chester, Pennsylvania. The new organization was formed after Boeing's Vertol division decided to give up marketing two of MBB's models in favor of concentrating more on its own products. The new subsidiary will handle sales and service for the United States, Canada, Mexico, and Central America from its Pennsylvania facilities.[55]

Soviet aircraft have also proven to be formidable competitors in the world helicopter market because the U.S.S.R. can grant financing terms no Western manufacturer can meet and because its helicopters have proven to be highly reliable. In the early 1970s a typical offer to an underdeveloped nation called for no down payment, 6 to 10 years to make the first payment, and interest rates as low as 2 percent.[56] U.S. officials maintain that the Soviets have in the past sold helicopters below cost to establish their position in markets where they were in competition with Western manufacturers.

Summary

For all of the reasons outlined in this chapter, U.S. producers argue that they have been forced to change their *modus operandi* and become leading multinationalists. In a market where the fastest growing segment lies abroad, co-production quotas, joint ventures, and offset agreements are increasingly seen as a business imperative, an exogenous constraint. Virtually all U.S. producers maintain they must produce abroad in order to sell abroad, regardless of the level of capacity utilization at home.

With both nationalized air carriers and manufacturers, not to mention a growing sense of Common Market cohesion, European governments have considerably increased their leverage against American manufacturers. But forecasts of a future European aircraft dominance to the contrary, the new market realities have pitted Yankee size and technology against European buying power. The result has been an international rapprochement: American-designed products made to a large degree by European labor. The chief loser appears to be the American production worker. It is indeed a problem of primary concern not only to New England and the West Coast, but to the rest of the nation as well. We shall return to this subject after we look at the question of capital investment and the spatial location of production.

Endnotes

1. Amarin Phillips, *Technology and Market Structure: A Study of the Aircraft Industry* (Lexington, Mass.: D. C. Heath, 1971), p. 30.
2. "Masters of the Air," *Time*, April 7, 1980, p. 54.
3. *Ibid.*
4. "McDonnell Douglas Is Flying Scared," *Fortune*, August 25, 1980, p. 42.
5. G. Christian Hill, "Lockheed Posts 2nd Quarter Loss of $26.6 Million," *Wall Street Journal*, July 30, 1980, p. 5.
6. Grant Winthrop, "A Rival Finally Comes Up to Speed," *Fortune*, December 17, 1979, p. 64.
7. *Ibid.*
8. *Census of Manufacturers, 1972*, Bureau of the Census, U.S. Department of Commerce. See also U.S. Congress, Subcommittee on Antitrust and Monopoly, Committee on Judiciary, Concentration Ratios in Manufacturing Industry, 1963, 89th Congress, 2nd Session, 1966.
9. Jeffrey Lenorovitz, "United CFM56 Selection Sparks DC-8 Retrofit," *Aviation Week*, April 9, 1979, p. 18.
10. Charles D. Bright, *The Jet Makers* (Lawrence, Kansas: Regents Press, 1979), pp. 93–95.
11. Howard Rudnitsky and Gerald Odening, "Jet Wars," *Forbes*, August 18, 1980, p. 35.
12. "GE President Sees Continuing Gains in Jet Engine Business," *Aviation Week*, December 27, 1965, p. 29.
13. *Ibid.*
14. *Forbes*, August 18, 1980, p. 35.
15. "General Electric Engines Ordered for A310," *Aviation Week*, August 25, 1980, p. 26.
16. William Carley, "United Technologies Plans New Engine for Jet Airplanes in a $1 Billion Project," *Wall Street Journal*, November 30, 1979, p. 14.
17. *Ibid.*
18. Richard O'Lone, "Pace of 757 Orders Raising Concern," *Aviation Week*, July 21, 1980, p. 43.
19. "The Rivalry Intensifies for Airbus Engines," *Business Week*, November 5, 1979, p. 68.
20. "Air France Postpones Decision on Powerplant for Airbus A310's," *Aviation Week*, October 8, 1979, p. 30.
21. *Ibid.*
22. "French Airline Selects CF6 for Its A310's," *Aviation Week*, December 31, 1979, p. 16.
23. Standard and Poor's, "Aerospace Basic Analysis," *Industry Surveys*, December 1, 1977 (Section 2), p. A15.
24. *Business Week*, August 6, 1966, p. 139.
25. *Wall Street Journal*, May 12, 1975, p. 26.
26. *Wall Street Journal*, June 30, 1975, p. 8.
27. David Boulton, "F-16: Sale of the Century" (Massachusetts: WGBH Education Foundation, 1979), p. 20.
28. David Griffiths, "Air Force Studies Impact of Engine Delivery Delay,"

Aviation Week, October 8, 1979, p. 22.

29. Winston Williams, "Engine Maker Works on Image," *New York Times*, December 26, 1979, p. D2.
30. Philip Geddes, "Giants Battle in U.S. Small Turbine Market," *Interavia*, March 1978, p. 180.
31. *Ibid.*
32. Anson Smith, "The GE Touch: Massachusetts Getting More Military Contracts Thanks to the Company's Winning Ways," *Boston Globe*, December 10, 1978, p. D8.
33. *Ibid.*
34. John Bell Rae, *Climb to Greatness: The American Aircraft Industry, 1920–1960* (Cambridge, Mass.: MIT Press, 1968), p. 204.
35. *Ibid.*, p. 205.
36. *Ibid.*, p. 205.
37. Philip Siekman, "The Big New Whirl in Helicopters," *Fortune*, April 1966, pp. 127–128.
38. *Ibid.*, p. 126.
39. *Ibid.*, p. 204.
40. *Ibid.*, p. 204.
41. "Sikorsky Contracted for Big Chopper," *Journal of Commerce*, December 24, 1976, p. 2.
42. *Ibid.*
43. "Will the Industry Sink into Obscurity After Vietnam," *New York Times*, August 20, 1975, p. F1.
44. Erwin J. Bulban, "Helicopter Market Growth Continues," *Aviation Week*, March 3, 1980, p. 219.
45. Standard and Poor's, "Aerospace Basic Analysis," p. A26.
46. Warren Wetmore, "Supplier Strikes Worry Engine Maker," *Aviation Week*, July 23, 1979, p. 23.
47. Unpublished special tabulations of the Dun & Bradstreet data were made available by David Birch, Laboratory for Neighborhood and Regional Change, Massachusetts Institute of Technology, May 1979.
48. Boulton, "F-16: Sale of the Century," p. 8.
49. "Sweeteners for Foreign Aircraft Sales," *Industry Week*, May 28, 1979, p. 87.
50. "A Drastic New Loss of Competitive Strength," *Business Week*, June 30, 1980, p. 58.
51. Jack Baranson, "Technology Transfer: Effects on U.S. Competitiveness and Employment," *The Impact of International Trade and Investment on Employment*, U.S. Department of Labor, 1978, p. 178.
52. Edward Kolcum, "Foreign Gains Threaten U.S. Lead," *Aviation Week*, November 27, 1978, p. 14.
53. Standard and Poor's, "Aerospace Basic Analysis," p. A23.
54. Erwin Bulban, "Helicopter Market Growth Continues," *Aviation Week*, March 3, 1980, p. 218.
55. *Ibid.*, p. 219.
56. "U.S. Pressed to Meet Helicopter Demand," *Aviation Week*, June 2, 1969, p. 344.

Chapter 5

CAPITAL INVESTMENT, PLANT LOCATION, AND TECHNOLOGY

Growing competition, stemming from both domestic and foreign sources, has compelled aircraft firms to continually re-evaluate their investment strategies, location decisions, and the technology they use. As history repeatedly suggests, no aircraft firm can expect to rest long on the strength of its past accomplishments. Constantly changing demands made by the military and the commercial airlines require perpetual investment in product research and the latest technology. Similarly, on-time production ultimatums and the increasing foreign demand for co-production and joint venture agreements dramatically affect where production now takes place. For individual firms within the aircraft industry, a single bad investment decision can mean billions of dollars in lost revenues and the loss of thousands of jobs as well.

Tracing the investment pattern of American industry is no simple matter, for much of the necessary information is confidential or of a proprietary nature. This is as true for aircraft as for most other industries, despite the fact that the aircraft industry derives so much of its revenue from the public sector. The government collects surprisingly few statistics on private capital flows, and even industry trade associations have little information on the investment decisions of their members. As a result it is necessary to pursue the subject with a combination of research tools: limited government statistics, newspaper accounts and journal articles, executive interviews, and periodically even some detective work to verify an industry rumor. Even more difficult than collecting

the statistics themselves is the task of interpreting industry motivation for a specific investment or production location decision.

Because of these obstacles, it is virtually impossible to trace the
investment patterns of the entire aircraft industry accurately. As
a result of our own location, we chose to focus on the New England
region and, in particular, on jet engine production. While we
cannot ascertain *a priori* whether the investment and location
decisions of the airframe manufacturers are closely allied to those
of the engine manufacturers, it seems certain that some of the
dynamics are similar. The location decisions are particularly important as they often largely determine the economic and social
fate of entire communities.

Aggregate Real Capital Investment

As expected, during the Viet-Nam-induced boom (1960–1968),
the rate of aggregate real gross investment in the New England
segment of the aircraft industry exploded. Mobilization required
massive new investment beginning in 1964 with a peak in 1966
and 1967. In both years real capital spending was nearly five times
the 1960 level. The installation of plant and equipment preceded
changes in value added and employment by approximately a year
during this period (see Figure 5.1). The sudden decline in war
spending left the industry with large amounts of unused capacity,
most of it privately financed in contrast to the situation following
World War II. Investment plummeted as sharply as it had risen.
Not until 1972 did the rate of investment begin to climb again.

When it did, the renewed investment was made largely to
modernize existing facilities, although investments were made in
new locations as well. One of the two aircraft turbine manufacturers recently completed a feasibility study to cost out a possible
move of its present plant to a southern state in line with the
migration of other industries to the Sunbelt. The study concluded
that it would take no less than 25 years to vacate its main New
England facility without disrupting production. The enormity of
sunk costs in existing aircraft facilities appears to preclude a capital
exodus, even if variable costs are substantially lower in the South.
However, for new facilities the location decision is much more
complicated. The same holds true, one would surmise, for large
airframe manufacturers on the West Coast.

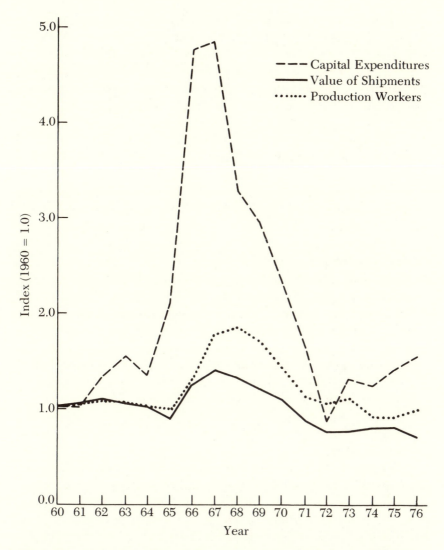

Figure 5.1 Growth in Capital Expenditures (Real), Value of Shipments (Real), and Number of Production Workers, 1960–1976, for New England Aircraft and Parts Industry (SIC 372) (all values indexed to 1960 = 1.0). Capital Expenditures deflated by the Capital Equipment PPI; Value of Shipments deflated by the Metal Products PPI (1967 = 100). (*Source: U.S. Bureau of the Census,* Annual Survey of Manufacturers, *1960–1976.*)

To pursue the question of industrial location in this industry, we have closely followed the investment activity of Pratt & Whitney, Hamilton-Standard, Sikorsky, and General Electric's Aircraft Engine Group. This investigation provides a key to understanding the nature of the investment decision process and the growing geographical dispersion of the industry's physical plant.

Expansion of the New England Aircraft Industry

United Technologies Corporation (UTC) has been New England's largest investor. Its Pratt & Whitney, Sikorsky, and Hamilton-Standard divisions, all headquartered in Connecticut, have expanded in the region along with its post–World War II investments in other geographic locations. Pratt & Whitney retains its division headquarters and largest physical plant in East Hartford where it was originally located in the late 1920s. At present the P&W structures in East Hartford include two massive manufacturing plants, an engineering facility, two administrative buildings, and an airport that accommodates wide-body transports. The division also operates four other facilities in Connecticut: North Haven, Rocky Hill, Middletown, and Southington. This last facility was leased from the federal government from 1950 to 1964, at which time it was purchased for $22 million. Jet engines are manufactured and overhauled within the massive 705,000-square-foot main plant.

The most recent round of expansion of these facilities began in the mid-1970s with new investment in the Southington plant. This was followed in 1976 with the addition to the East Hartford complex of a $3.5 million laboratory for the testing of engine control components.[1] A year later an $18 million addition to the Middletown facility was completed for engine research,[2] followed by a $12 million capital improvement to the Wilgoos turbine lab, also part of the East Hartford complex.[3] Today, the costly lab is the largest privately owned turbine test facility in the world.

Pratt & Whitney's most recent capital expansion, however, occurred outside of Connecticut. In early 1979 it purchased an existing 824,000-square-foot plant in North Berwick, Maine, for $9 million.[4] This new acquisition is being used for vane and blade production, which at one time was done exclusively in the North Haven facility. Originally, Pratt & Whitney planned to spend

$10 million on plant improvement and about $20 million for equipment. In December 1979, however, P&W announced that it would spend an additional $57 million to increase manufacturing capacity and productivity at the Maine plant.[5] The investment, largely in machine tools and other equipment, is being made to help speed the delivery of engines and spare parts and to help prepare for the production phase of P&W's 2037 turbine, still three to four years away.

In addition to the North Berwick expansion, P&W also intends to spend $46 million on machine tools for its five Connecticut facilities, again to facilitate timely delivery of both its military and commercial products.[6]

All of Pratt & Whitney's central Connecticut facilities specialize in the manufacture of large turbine engines, particularly the JT8D, JT9D, and F100. The North Berwick facility marks the first capital expansion for this purpose outside of the Connecticut area. The reason for this shift in investment strategy is discussed later in the chapter. Apparently pleased with the expansion to rural Maine, P&W's parent firm, United Technologies, announced late in 1980 that it would expand its manufacturing capacity still further by building new plants in Georgia and South Carolina.

While Pratt & Whitney has only recently begun to expand its large turbine production facilities outside Connecticut, its extra-regional growth has been extensive, but restricted to product lines other than large turbines. Small jet engines and parts for general aviation aircraft are manufactured by a wholly owned subsidiary, Pratt & Whitney of Canada. In 1962 the company acquired a second Canadian plant in St. Hubert, adjacent to its original Longueuil, Quebec, facility. In 1971 a third plant was built for the production of small turbines. It was located in West Virginia, according to company officials, because of this site's proximity to both markets and suppliers, a good airport and highway system, its labor pool, and the receptivity of the state government.[7] How much each of these factors weighed in the final location decision is not easily ascertained.

The largest Pratt & Whitney site in terms of physical size is in West Palm Beach, Florida, a complex covering over 10 square miles used for the testing, development, and production of atmospheric and space propulsion systems. First built in the mid-1950s, it was expanded to accommodate military testing operations in 1967, and then expanded again during the mid-1970s. The choice of this location had little to do with labor costs or transportation networks; the most important locational attribute of the site was its distance from population centers, because of the tremendous noise generated by rocket engine tests. No consideration was ever given to locating this facility in the heavily populated Northeast.

Pratt & Whitney's sister division, Hamilton-Standard, is more centralized with virtually all of its aerospace facilities located on a single 320-acre tract of land in Windsor Locks, Connecticut, adjacent to Bradley Field Airport. As a propeller manufacturer, it dates back to 1919, but after World War II the division began to diversify its aircraft product line and eventually moved into electronics and automotive diagnostic equipment in an attempt to shield itself from the aerospace business cycle. Following its parent firm's propensity for acquisition, Hamilton-Standard acquired AMBAC Corporation in 1978, a geographically dispersed producer of electronic fuel injection systems. In so doing, Hamilton-Standard acquired plants in Michigan, Massachusetts, Mississippi, Illinois, Pennsylvania, New York, and California. The specialized vendor support required in its propeller and aircraft parts production, however, has precluded the company from moving its aerospace division from its present location. It therefore continues to expand and modernize in New England.

UTC's Sikorsky Aircraft division has also been a significant investor in the region. Until recently, the firm had maintained all of its production in a single plant in Connecticut, on a 254-acre tract in Stratford. During the early 1970s the company acquired a second manufacturing plant and a set of office buildings on a 35-acre tract in Bridgeport, Connecticut.

After the division won the UTTAS competition and was awarded the Army contract to manufacture 1,100 Black Hawk helicopters, it announced plans to award $1 billion in subcontracts. Two months after that announcement in March 1977, however, the company made the unprecedented decision to bring a large proportion of the production in-house. Sikorsky allegedly made this decision when studies by the division showed that vendors might not be capable of meeting future delivery requirements demanded by the UTTAS contract. Outside suppliers will continue to manufacture small quantities of transmission components to assure Sikorsky of second-source capability in the event of an emergency.

The decision to transfer engine transmission production inside involved constructing and equipping a new plant at its Stratford military products complex. The new plant is designed for complete production from beginning to end. Sikorsky expects to build 1,500 Black Hawk helicopter transmissions in the new facility over the course of the next several years and to produce approximately seven transmission systems per month for the commercial S-76.[8]

The cost of the project is estimated to be in excess of $10 million, which covers construction of the plant and installation of about a hundred pieces of manufacturing equipment.[9] The new plant will employ the latest material handling and production flow technology to enable the division to meet the Army's delivery schedule. Numerically controlled machine tools are prominent among the equipment that Sikorsky has purchased.

In addition to constructing this new plant, Sikorsky has been in the midst of a major $100 million plant expansion and modernization program since the late 1970s.[10] With the Defense Department's enormous procurement plans and the staggering success of the company's S-76 in the commercial market, Sikorsky's production schedule contemplates manufacture of nearly 300 helicopters annually by 1982 and an average of 330 per year by 1986.[11] In comparison, Sikorsky produced only 15 helicopters in 1977 and 33 units in 1978.[12] This expansion is likely to be beneficial for southern Connecticut's aircraft labor force, as the division has indicated that employment in the main Stratford plant alone may reach 11,500 by the end of 1981, an increase of 2,000 workers from 1978.

While Sikorsky's plans call for large amounts of capital spending within the region, the division, like P&W, has also begun to pursue extra-regional expansion for the first time. Plants are being built in West Palm Beach, Florida, and Long Beach, California, to facilitate assembly and service of S-76 helicopters. These plants are said to be the first of a network of S-76 support centers around the world[13] and will provide Sikorsky with some backup or parallel facilities for assembly and maintenance of its civilian helicopters. In so doing, it follows the lead of other aircraft firms.

Parallel Production Facilities in the Aircraft Industry

For UTC, the Pratt & Whitney expansion into Maine marks the. first real attempt by the company to establish parallel production facilities. But well before UTC began to build parallel facilities, General Electric had geographically dispersed its Aircraft Engine Group in similar fashion to other company divisions. Following World War II, GE began to decentralize the overall organization according to product line, type of work, and management responsibility. The company's objective was to operate each "decentralized business venture to achieve its own customer acceptance and profitable results, by taking the appropriate business risks."[14]

Today, GE's operations are highly decentralized and are organized into six sectors, each of which is largely a separate enterprise. Each sector is both a management and planning organization and is made up of a number of Strategic Business Units (SBUs). The Aircraft Engine Group is one such SBU. Although the parent company provides much of the finance capital for the division's R&D and new plant and equipment, the group is expected, in the long run, to pay its own way.

Unlike its competitor, GE's aircraft turbine capacity is divided between its Lynn–Everett works in Massachusetts and its large Evendale, Ohio, plant outside of Cincinnati. The criterion for this separation is based on the size of the engines produced. Final assembly of large aircraft engines is accomplished at the Evendale plant, while Lynn is equipped to assemble smaller turbines. Parts for both types of engines, however, are produced at the two facilities, providing a degree of parallel capacity.

Moreover, in pursuing these strategies of expansion and parallel production, General Electric has been able to disperse its production facilities throughout the nation. For example, since the 1960s it has acquired production facilities in Massachusetts and Vermont and established its own manufacturing facilities in Albuquerque, New Mexico, and Madisonville, Kentucky. One of its newer Massachusetts plants, once an abandoned furniture factory, is used to build in-flight aviation equipment. Its expansion into Vermont in the mid-1970s entailed construction of a new

80,000-square-foot plant in Rutland. According to one source, the company's overt satisfaction with the productivity of the local labor force (mostly women) led it to begin expansion of this plant in 1979. According to a GE spokesman, the growing demand for commercial power plants was the motivating factor behind the addition. At the time of the announcement, the company predicted that the Rutland expansion would create 300 to 500 jobs and would increase total GE employment in the area to over 1,000 workers.[15] This makes GE one of the largest employers in the area.

Additional plans for AEG expansion were made public in December 1979, when the division announced its intention to establish a facility in Madisonville, Kentucky, to forge and cast airfoils.[16] The new plant will initially manufacture turbine blades and vanes for one of GE's military turbines, and capacity will be added at a later date for the division's CF6-50 and CFM56 commercial jet engines. The new operation will be housed in an existing 50,000-square-foot plant at Madisonville that previously manufactured parts for another GE division. GE indicated that employment would likely reach 200 by the end of 1980, with some of the previous Madisonville employees being retained for aircraft parts production through state-sponsored training programs.

In expanding its division to new and generally non-unionized areas, General Electric's AEG mirrors Pratt & Whitney's expansion to North Berwick, Maine. In a period when reducing the probability of production disruption is viewed as a business imperative, both aircraft giants are more actively pursuing expansion outside the industrial Northeast. Indeed, the threat of having engine deliveries halted by vendor or in-house work stoppages has encouraged the movement of production facilities to areas outside of union influence. The latest General Electric expansions came in the wake of lengthy strikes at two of its critical vendors, one of which was a major forging manufacturer. In responding to the issue of late deliveries caused by these strikes, one General Electric official commented, "Like others in the aircraft engine business, we are concerned about strikes at some of our major suppliers. . . . We're managing the problem and to date have met all delivery schedules. We are investigating alternate sources. . . ."[17] It appears that GE concluded from its analysis that the most reliable source for these jet engine components would be its own manufacturing facility within the AEG network, but in a non-union area.

This movement, beginning in the 1960s, marks the first real departure from the time-honored industry strategy of reinvesting in existing facilities and locations. Recall that after World War II virtually all of the major aircraft firms that had expanded into the interior of the country returned to their original locations to take advantage of their most productive facilities. Today the centrifugal forces engendered in the parallel production strategy seem to be eclipsing the centripetal forces of agglomeration and scale economies.

Investment, Disinvestment, Location, and Acquisition in the Subcontractor Network

The investment and location experience of the supplier firms is considerably different from that of the primes. The diminished level of subcontract orders following Viet-Nam, combined with the end of the last commercial re-equipment drive, forced many regional vendors out of business. This was particularly true of the very smallest shops, as noted in the last chapter. Many of them fell victim to increased make/buy ratios and multiple sourcing, creating a good deal of resentment in the vendor community. Others were prey to acquisition by larger concerns when they faced capital financing constraints. One small New England supplier complained to us that eventually he will be forced to sell his company, despite the fact that his firm is doing well at the present time.

> In the next five to ten years, we will be bought up by a bigger company because we will reach the end of our financial rope. If you do not grow, you die. Our only chance is to merge with someone who has more financial prowess than we do. Small companies are bought up because they cannot get enough financial help to grow.

Ownership in the subcontractor network changes hands for other reasons as well. A particularly good example involves one of New England's oldest and once independent suppliers of jet engine parts that currently employs 600 workers. The firm began as a four-person shop in the mid-1930s when its main products were tools and fixtures used by the aircraft industry. World War II provided the impetus for its success, as the firm was involved in the production of parts for the widely used Pratt & Whitney "Wasp" engine. The firm also did extremely well during Viet-Nam, when its workforce reached 1,800.

In 1968 the original owners sold out to a large multinational machine tool company headquartered in Michigan in order for them to "reap some enjoyment in their retirement." From their standpoint it was a perspicacious transaction, for a company spokesman named 1971 as the most unprofitable year since 1960: "We went down with the rest of the industry." The original owner/ managers continued to operate the plant under contract for five years, at which time the parent brought in its own management team. In this case the transaction merely involved a change in ownership, and no relocation of physical capacity transpired.

In another case, however, involving a large Boston area parts manufacturer, acquisition entailed immediate disinvestment. Until a few years ago this firm fabricated metal parts for both automobile and aircraft engines. Its aircraft division had reached a critical point where management felt the division had to grow or be sold. Based on the volatility of the aircraft parts market, management decided to sell the division to a large mid-western concern and concentrate on what appeared (at least at the time) to be the more "stable" automobile sector. The acquiring multi-unit firm had a similar operation in Ohio and chose to consolidate its aircraft-related production there. Some of the workers affected by the transfer of ownership moved to Ohio; most senior employees bumped workers with lower seniority in the auto parts division.

The Location Decision for the Subcontractor

Other vendors have adapted to the volatility of the aircraft market in a variety of ways. During periods of contraction, some vendors have reacted with the selective phasing out of specific activities, while a few have attempted to convert their production facilities to other uses. In periods of expansion, plant relocation has been common in order to obtain increased space or to tap a new labor market. Almost all such relocation is intra-regional, however, with most moves being restricted to a nearby community.

One small, but expanding firm located in Massachusetts provides a good example. It began operations in Brookline in 1958 and moved to larger leased quarters six miles away in Newton in 1962. By 1978 it had outgrown this facility as well, and the owner sought to build his own plant. He indicated that he would have built in Newton if it were not for the high local property tax, but he never seriously considered leaving the state.

We're identified with Massachusetts. We could have gone to New Hampshire; however, it won't be long before these other states are faced with the same problems as Massachusetts. As new industries move into these areas, the need for services (police, fire, roads, schools) will all have to go up.

We thought of going across the border to New Hampshire. But for what reason? We figured it out and for a company our size, it doesn't mean much. For one thing we can't get the people we want up there. We can't afford to lose all our staff. Our company is made up of people who have to think. Our company is people.

The site eventually chosen was in Worcester County, Massachusetts, about 40 minutes west of Newton. The main considerations were accessibility to major markets, the availability of skilled labor, and access to a good highway system.

Other small vendors in southern New England who have survived cite similar reasons for remaining in the region. They include the existence of a skilled labor force that "knows how to build aircraft engine parts and thinks in three dimensions," a good highway transportation network, and an area that offers a variety of cultural and recreational activities.

The above factors appear to be the most important in explaining the continuing capital investments of New England aircraft machine shops. For the newer, high-technology suppliers, dependent on sophisticated research and development activities, the region remains attractive because of its universities, especially MIT. Although the costs of labor, taxes, energy, and transportation are important, they are not the primary criteria in the investment/location decision. The vice president of a missile and space industry subcontractor was explicit on this score.

The Northeast has historically been a pretty good location for engineering people. Certainly, places in the country that may be very cost effective from a standpoint of taxes or housing costs, or other cost factors, wouldn't be attractive unless they were the kind of places you could get technical people to come to. Right now the average salary in this place is $20,000 a year. If it was an expansion in the production direction, of course, there would be one set of sites that might be acceptable. If it was in the engineering direction there would be another.

For this firm the level of new capital investment in its Massachusetts facility is strictly a function of its degree of success in winning NASA and Defense Department contracts. Success in this regard depends on technical and political factors, not on relative tax burdens, labor costs, or other direct expenses of doing business. Again the standard relative cost explanations of neo-classical economic theory appear to be of little value in understanding the aircraft location decision.

Most of the vendors that fail in New England usually do so not because of high cost or poor quality, but as a result of decisions made by prime contractors beyond the control of the individual vendor. In this sense the level of capital investment within the regional vendor network is almost exclusively the outcome of a host of factors related to the aircraft business cycle and complex international marketing and production arrangements. Disinvestment rarely occurs through out-migration; it happens through plant closings, and in some cases, horizontal and conglomerate acquisition.

A Special Case of Relocation: Pratt & Whitney's Move to Maine

The motivation behind specific investment and location decisions is often hard to uncover. This is best illustrated by Pratt & Whitney's acquisition of its North Berwick, Maine, facility. Why P&W chose this particular site 180 miles from East Hartford is a matter of extensive controversy. The original explanation given by the parent corporation was that the current boom in aircraft required P&W to add capacity immediately and therefore seek out an existing facility with appropriate physical characteristics.[18] In the final analysis, the North Berwick site and a site in Lancaster, Pennsylvania, were considered after 20 sites in Connecticut were investigated, but found "unacceptable."

The state of Maine offered $2.1 million in tax abatements, ostensibly to attract P&W to North Berwick. A wage differential estimated as $1.50 to $2.00 per hour for semi-skilled machinists has also been mentioned as a determinant of this particular location decision.

Both the tax abatement and wage differential incentives may have played some role in the final choice of the Maine site, but it is difficult to maintain that they were the determining factors. Given the initial $39 million investment in the plant, $2.1 million in tax savings over the life of the facility must be seen as a minor consideration. The wage differential between central Connecticut and Maine may be a greater inducement, but given the low ratio of production worker payroll to value added in the industry (29 percent in 1976),[19] the wage differential amounts to no more than a difference of 7.3 percent in unit cost for the particular components manufactured there.* Moreover, these components comprise only a tiny fraction of the cost of a complete engine, so that the labor savings as a percent of total cost is indeed miniscule.

What adds to the mystery about this particular location decision is the apparent surplus of plant capacity in East Hartford. In 1967, during the war-induced boom, as many as 22,000 workers were employed in the East Hartford plant. At the beginning of 1979 only 11,000 were working in the same facility. While there has been no contraction of the physical plant itself, P&W chose not to expand production there. Several industry sources suggest that the skill shortage in Connecticut, not the shortage of physical capacity, was the ultimate reason for the move to Maine. According to this argument, the company refused to compete further with its own subcontractors for existing skilled labor, and it felt that the Hartford area's unskilled pool lacked the discipline and basic education to warrant vocational training paid for by the company.

This explanation does not clear up the mystery, however. A shortage of fully trained and experienced aircraft workers is a serious problem in the Hartford area, but it appears that North Berwick does not provide any more of a skilled labor pool. In addition, the unemployment rate in North Berwick was low at the time of the purchase. In the words of one concerned town resident, "North Berwick already has two jobs for every worker in town."[20] Other observers of the move suggested that P&W would have to recruit workers from New Hampshire and still other workers would have to be lured from smaller companies in the local area. Skilled workers were transferred from Hartford to Maine in order to train new workers there. For these reasons it is difficult to maintain that P&W chose North Berwick to escape the skilled labor crunch in Connecticut.

The one remaining plausible explanation for the North Berwick choice goes to the heart of the parallel production strategy. Given the industry's heightened competition over on-time contract performance, P&W may have chosen the non-union Maine location

---

* This calculation is based on a 25-percent hourly wage differential ($6.00 versus $8.00) and the 29-percent production wages/value-added ratio.

to assure continuous production in the event of labor disruption in the unionized North Haven facility. Referring to the P&W move, Hadley P. Atlass, Director of Maine's State Development Office, stated that he anticipated no "union problems" in the new facility.[21]

Adding even more credence to this view is the fact that P&W announced a large capital expenditure program (involving $57 million) for the Maine facility soon after its military engine deliveries were slowed by labor strikes at two of its vendors. The company was under severe pressure from the Defense Department to speed up its deliveries of engines for F-15 and F-16 fighters. In order to ensure its dominant position in this market segment, P&W may have found it necessary to increase manufacturing capacity within its own network rather than risk additional delays in engine deliveries by expanding its vendor base.

The North Berwick mystery thus contains too many suspects, and as in Agatha Christie's "Murder on the Orient Express," they may *all* be implicated. Some observers have suggested the following as a plausible scenario: P&W management initially decided on a site outside of central Connecticut in order to escape the severe labor shortage in the area and to circumvent the union organization there. Rather than initiating a large-scale training program in the Hartford area, management chose to seek out an alternative labor force that was more easily trainable and perhaps less motivated to affiliate with organized labor. Once the decision to leave Connecticut was made, the final decision to approve the Maine site over Pennsylvania may have been determined on the basis of wage, tax, and transportation cost differentials. From the perspective of management this may be a completely rational decision, despite the objections of labor and community groups in the Hartford area. The location decision—at least in the aircraft industry—has become a highly charged and complex political-economic issue.

Diversification and Conversion

Investment in new productive facilities is not the only course for the leading aerospace firms. The highly cyclical nature of the aircraft market has influenced and often forced prime contractors and their suppliers to carry out both diversification and conversion efforts. It is important to note that the two strategies are not synonymous. Conversion occurs when a *given* plant or facility changes over from the production of one set of commodities to another. A shift from defense-related work to non-defense activity is often entailed. In contrast, diversification involves the redeployment of financial capital into related or unrelated markets by means of investment in *new* facilities or by merger or acquisition.

Numerous examples of diversification can be identified. The most extensive involves the acquisition behavior of UTC. As late as 1973 sales to the U.S. government were responsible for 46 percent of total UTC revenue.[22] With the acquisition of the Essex Group in 1974, Otis Elevator in 1975, and AMBAC/American Bosch in 1978, the government share of sales dropped below 27 percent.[23] With a broader base of revenues from diverse industrial and commercial sectors, UTC argues that it is "better equipped to weather business cycles and economic swings."[24] Industrial products were responsible for over 40 percent of UTC's 1977 revenue and half of its operating profit. Four years earlier virtually all profit and revenue came from its power division (jet turbine/ rocket) and from flight systems (helicopters) (see Table 5.1).

This conglomerate expansion strategy very likely improves the long-run stability and profitability of the company, but its impact on the viability of its home base—in this case, New England—is somewhat controversial. What is good for the company may not necessarily be optimal from the point of view of the community. Virtually none of the production facilities of the Essex Group or Otis Elevator are located in the region, nor is there any indication by UTC's central management of an intention to move facilities there. Only one AMBAC division is located in New England (Springfield, Massachusetts). Consequently, there has been no net employment growth in the region as a result of these acquisitions valued at over $1.1 billion in 1977.[25] In the long run, such conglomerate diversification may even harm the region if capital resources generated from the power and flight system divisions are diverted to these new industrial acquisitions or used for acquiring other firms at the expense of power and flight expansion. The delay in making a full-scale financial commitment to the JT10D turbine actually may have been partly caused by this factor, although in this case the company seems to have successfully recovered from the delay.

Small firms seldom have the economic resources required to

Table 5.1 Diversification of United Technologies Corporation, Distribution of Revenues, Profits, and Assets: 1973 vs. 1977

	Revenues		Profits		Identifiable Assets	
	1973	1977	1973	1977	1973	1977
Power Systems	76.7%	45.4%	51.2%	40.1%	73.5%	28.6%
Flight Systems	21.7	11.2	50.6	10.3	12.1	9.6
Industrial Products	—	42.2	—	49.5	—	38.0
Other	1.5	1.1	-1.8	0.1	14.4	23.8

SOURCE: UTC 1977 Annual Report, "Consolidated Summary of Business Segment Data."

diversify through acquisition. Instead, within the subcontractor network, there are a number of noteworthy cases of conversion. One former manufacturer of STOL (Short Take-Off & Landing) aircraft with engineering facilities in Massachusetts and production facilities near Wichita, Kansas, was driven out of the aircraft business by a series of bizarre circumstances allegedly involving the Central Intelligence Agency. Faced with imminent bankruptcy, the owners sold the airplane firm in 1976 and used the proceeds to start an aerospace subcontracting business. The converted firm still produces for the Defense Department, but instead of light aircraft, its products embody a high degree of advanced engineering in landing gear components and specialized military aircraft doors. In two years, sales rose from $750,000 to $3 million and employment doubled.

The outstanding example of conversion in New England, and perhaps in the entire nation, involves the Kaman Corporation of Bloomfield, Connecticut. Until 1965 Kaman was a prime contractor for the Defense Department, producing turbine-powered helicopters. Unable to compete effectively with Sikorsky and Bell because of its inability to take advantage of scale economies and because of the uncertainty of military orders, Kaman's management sought ways to apply its aerospace technology to commercial production. In this extraordinary case, the musical interests of the firm's president led the company to design an acoustic guitar that now successfully competes with Japanese imports. To accomplish this feat, the firm borrowed extensively from its helicopter technology. Most engineers in this field are vibration specialists, for vibration is the helicopter's major drawback. Since sound is no more than high-frequency vibration, Kaman's engineers were able to utilize their skills to design a more effective sound box for the guitar. The corporation was also an innovator in fiberglass laminates used in helicopter rotor blades. This technology was also successfully adapted to guitar construction. The firm has now entered the alternative energy field with a number of windmill prototypes. In both of these remarkable instances the corporation has successfully dealt with the most difficult problem of conversion, namely, the retraining of the existing labor force to produce commercially marketable products. By 1977 Kaman's share of revenues from aerospace was down to less than 15 percent of its $215 million in sales; government contracts had declined to less than 19 percent.[26] Meanwhile Kaman was able to maintain employment at nearly 3,300, the same level as in 1973.

As a means of retaining employment in a region, conversion of the capital base is clearly superior to diversification by acquisition. The few cases of successful conversion provide the exception rather than the rule, however. Most defense contractors are technically and managerially ill equipped to make the transition to the non-aircraft commercial market. Boeing-Vertol's foray into the light rail vehicle (LRV) market, for example, ended up in near disaster when its first customer, the Massachusetts Bay Transit Authority in Boston, found the Boeing LRVs so technologically complex that they could not be maintained in regular service. As a result the city successfully sued Boeing, and the company subsequently dropped out of this specialized market. The recent case of broken frames on city buses manufactured by Grumman aircraft provides another example of the difficulty in making a successful conversion to commercial products. Product and occupational incompatibility as well as institutional differences between commercial sales and defense contracting provide significant hurdles that even firms like Boeing have been unable to overcome.

Sources of Finance

The government obviously plays a critical role in all aspects of the aircraft industry. The intimate relationship between the federal government and the industry is nowhere more evident than in the financing of plant, equipment, and working capital. Although the recent trend has been to wean the industry from its absolute dependence on the public sector, it still relies on the government for a major share of its income and even for the factories in which many aircraft and turbine engines are built.

The Government's Role

From World War II until 1957, it was common practice for the federal government to furnish prime contractors with fully equipped plants, the rationale being that private capital would be unwilling to invest sufficient funds if the additional undepreciated capacity might have no profitable use after demobilization. In 1957 the government changed its policy and began to encourage private firms to buy the plants outright. These attempts were generally rebuffed, however, because the prevailing long-term lease arrangements were so profitable to the industry. They permit prime contractors to produce goods without tying up valuable capital assets and also allow them to avoid local property taxes on these exempted facilities. Some lease arrangements even allow firms to produce up to 25 percent non-defense goods in federally owned plants, providing additional incentive to lease rather than own the plant. Besides shipbuilding, no other industry enjoys this implicit government subsidy.

Today, several aircraft firms still use federally owned plant space on a lease basis. General Electric's Everett, Massachusetts, facility covering 49 acres and 350,000 square feet of plant space was constructed by the U.S. government in 1941 at an original acquisition cost of $9.7 million.[27] It is still wholly owned by the Air Force, which has unsuccessfully recommended expediting negotiations for the sale of the plant to GE. Besides production of military jet engines at the plant, parts for the commercial CF6 are manufactured in the facility. The replacement cost of the site was valued at $37 million in 1977. The Air Force also continues to own 18 of the 61 acres of the GE Lynn site, recently valued at $68 million. This facility has also been recommended for sale, but GE has expressed no interest whatsoever in its purchase. The lease arrangement is clearly more profitable.

In another instance, Boeing leases a plant in Kansas. This facility, which was built in the early 1940s, includes 69 buildings, 5 million square feet of floor space, and 66,000 pieces of machinery and equipment.[28] Boeing uses these facilities to produce aircraft equipment and spare parts. Whereas many government attempts to sell such plants to private industry have failed, the General Services Administration (GSA) announced its intention in December 1979 to sell the plant to Boeing for $44.8 million after nearly 40 years of government ownership. Boeing's need for commercial production space makes this purchase profitable for the first time. The once-favorable lease arrangement and now the direct sale of manufacturing assets provide a very special investment source to the aircraft industry.

Unlike plant and equipment, working capital is provided to prime contractors through another mechanism, progress payments—remittances by the government of portions of the total contract obligation while work is still in progress. These payments do not come solely from the public sector, however. Commercial sector progress payments are usually provided by the air carriers in the course of their purchases and leases. Until the Boeing 747 program, these civilian progress payments were of smaller magnitude than military percentages, but the sheer size of the 747 commitment forced a change in this system. For this program, airlines made periodic progress payments in the two years prior to delivery of aircraft amounting to 50 percent of the total costs.[29] For military work before 1957, the advance payment percentages were 100 percent on cost-plus and 80 percent on fixed-price contracts.[30] Since 1957 these percentages have been scaled down depending on the size and type of contract. Nevertheless, progress payments are still a major consideration in the pursuit of government work.

With the growth of the commercial sector and the declining role of the federal government (especially in providing production facilities), even some of the largest airframe manufacturers have found it necessary to turn to the private long-term debt market to finance new physical capacity. Before the early 1950s, most prime contractors in the industry utilized little long-term debt to finance their activities. Between 1941 and 1953, the major airframe companies issued only $8.7 million worth of bonds and preferred common stock.[31] A high level of investment was undertaken by the firms in the mid and late 1950s, however, largely as a result of the rise of missilery and the new facilities needed for their development and production. Much of this investment had to be privately financed. This was accomplished through the long-term debt market. The 16 manufacturers that had issued only $8.7 million of debt and equity over 12 years issued $256 million in bonds between 1953 and 1958 alone.[32] Thus, a pattern of external financing was established that contrasted sharply with the pre-1953 practice.

Financial Risk and Business Risk

This greater use of financial leverage has added a new risk dimension to the industry. As one close observer put it, historically,[33]

> . . . the industry has relied upon short-term debt to avoid financial problems which might come during periods of little military spending, but this relatively secure system of the past has given way to a new period of greater danger because of increased capital expenditures based on long-term debt. . . .

In turning to the bond market, according to financial community experts, the airframe sector has invoked unsound business practices by superimposing a high financial risk upon a high business risk. This new strategy is partially responsible for the fiscal problems that have plagued some of the airframe manufacturers, Lockheed in particular.

Jet engine producers have apparently avoided this problem. General Electric's Aircraft Engine Group relies on the parent company to provide finance capital for much of its R&D and new plant and equipment, although the AEG and all other divisions are considered independent profit centers that in the long run are expected to provide all of the retained earnings for this purpose. UTC operates in a similar manner, utilizing little long-term debt; in 1977 the company boasted a 0.18 to 1 debt/equity ratio.[34]

Yet for many firms, internal financing is not feasible, and with the decline in the domestic military market, both airframe and turbine manufacturers have been forced to find other sources of capital. The commercial debt market is normally precluded for basic R&D work, for it is considered to be extremely high risk. Moreover, the equity market will seldom accommodate a venture stock issue large enough to provide the necessary funds for production tooling. Consequently, more and more of the major primes experiencing capital constraints have gone abroad to form joint ventures with foreign firms and governments. The GE/SNECMA agreement on the CFM56 turbine is just one example of this type of capital-sharing arrangement.

Under the agreement, GE provided the technology for the compressor portion of the engine, originally developed for the B-1 bomber, and SNECMA contributed half of the necessary capital. GE argued that it needed the French money to help develop the engine for the commercial market because it could not undertake the cost of development on its own.[35] According to industry sources, federal anti-trust laws make it difficult for domestic firms to enter into joint ventures among themselves, therefore providing an incentive for the proliferation of these foreign contacts. The price to domestic firms for obtaining capital in this way is shared profit; the price to the economy is the export of jobs and technology.

Capital Finance in the Subcontractor Network

In general, smaller subcontractors have access to none of the financial resources available to the primes: government-owned facilities, progress payments, guaranteed government loans, and joint ventures. They are, therefore, often compelled to enter the debt market to finance new plant and equipment, raw material purchases, and other forms of working capital when past retained earnings are insufficient to cover expenses. In many cases, given the high failure rate in this industry segment, banks are unwilling to make any funds available. When they are, some subcontractors complain that the price is exhorbitant. One outraged owner commented,

> *The banks collateralize the hell out of us, despite what you hear about the big banks wanting to help us. We can't raise capital by selling stock. No one would buy it. And we can't borrow at a decent rate. Our interest charges are greater than our earnings.*
>
> *We are crunched by the banks. We cannot get enough capital. With more capital we could expand our machine shop and bring some of our stuff inside rather than buy from the outside. We don't have enough retained earnings to invest.*

Most of the small firms interviewed in New England reported that they are able to persuade banks to finance only inventory or accounts receivable (that is, short-term debt); long-term debt and venture capital for plant expansion are almost non-existent, they claim. Given their size, these firms are also unable to enter into joint ventures. As a result, they are often the reluctant victims of acquisition by larger concerns.

Another common complaint among vendors is that local banks in particular are not responsive to their needs. One subcontractor from Hartford said he was forced to do business with banks from New York City and Boston because local banks "don't loan money" and "don't move fast enough." Another large Hartford area firm claimed that it has access to the local banks only for short-term finance requirements. For its long-term capital needs, it uses large insurance companies and banks located in Nebraska, North Carolina, and California.

Thus, as in the case of markets and competition, the financing arrangements of smaller subcontractors bear little resemblance to those of the primes, despite their interdependence. The special nature of competition and problems of finance in the industry place vendors in a precarious position, even when their cost structures are competitive. Once again the subcontractors turn out to be the tail on the industry dog.

Operations, Technology, and Supplies

Beyond the area of finance, actual production technologies are an important consideration in the aircraft industry. The sector's traditional dependence on well-paid, highly skilled labor has continually induced managers to innovate in this sphere. According to Charles Kirby of General Electric's AEG,[36]

> *Ever-increasing labor costs, manpower shortages, and decreasing cycle time to develop and produce new products make it mandatory to be constantly alert for new techniques or developments which will increase productivity, technical advancement of the product, or improvement in quality.*

The fact that aircraft products themselves have always been at the forefront of technological improvement has special implications for the development of new production methods.

Years ago, most innovation was directed toward physical plant facilities. As planes grew in size, buildings were needed that could accommodate cranes, winches, and scaffolding within the structures themselves. This was primarily a West Coast phenomenon where airframes were being fabricated. During World War II, when production runs irrevocably increased in size, the emphasis was placed upon mass production and the layout of the typical plant became more "process" oriented. This trend applied to the eastern component manufacturers as well as to the western airframe producers.

Since that era the industry's efforts in technological improvement have focused upon the machine tools used in production. When interviewed, nearly all industry spokespersons cited the use of more advanced machinery, fewer production workers, and an increasingly specialized workforce as major operations changes.

Much of the new machinery is of the numerically controlled (NC) type developed substantially during the late 1950s and introduced on a wide scale during the 1960s and early 1970s. With the introduction of NC equipment, the machining process was radically altered. Instead of depending totally on the skills of the individual machinist, the process involves the feeding of numerical data directly into the machine tool to control the actions of the machinery. By 1976 almost one fourth of all new machine tool purchases by the aircraft industry were of the NC variety, a pro-

Table 5.2　Percentage of New Machine Tool Purchases for Numerically Controlled Machine Tools

Purchasing Industry	Metal-Cutting Machine Tools	Metal-Forming Machine Tools
Metalworking Machinery (SIC 354)	8.1%	0.3%
Railroad Equipment (SIC 374)	10.1	2.4
Construction and Mining Machinery (SIC 353)	15.3	3.0
Ordnance and Accessories (SIC 348)	15.5	1.2
Guided Missiles, Space Vehicles (SIC 376)	18.0	2.7
Aircraft and Parts (SIC 372)	23.4	2.2

SOURCE: *12th American Machinist Inventory of Metalworking Equipment 1976–1978*. Reprinted from Glynnis Trainer, *The Metalworking Machinery Industry in New England: An Analysis of Investment Behavior*, Joint Center for Urban Studies, MIT–Harvard, August 1979, p. 138.

portion far in excess of all other leading industries that utilize them (see Table 5.2).

The industry is the dominant user in part because the machines, the brainchild of a Sikorsky subcontractor, were originally developed for the production of aircraft and missile parts. Between 1949 and 1959 the Air Force spent at least $62 million on their development, thus contributing in still another way to the industry.[37]

Over the past two decades, NC technology has been commercially developed in a variety of ways. Computerized numerical control (CNC), for example, is a development in which a mini-computer is placed directly on the machine tool to control the production process. Direct numerical control (DNC) is the newest addition to the line of NC equipment. Under a DNC system several machine tools are controlled by a single computer, thereby eliminating the need for "stand-alone" numerically controlled equipment.

McDonnell Douglas, the most extensive user of DNC equipment in the United States, has been expanding its use of DNC at a staggering pace. Between 1975 and 1977 the McDonnell Aircraft division of the corporation doubled the number of machine tools operating under DNC in its machining plants, and its commitment to the concept has been growing larger each year.[38] The DNC system in St. Louis alone was to be expanded by one fifth in the two-year period 1979–1980, and the company's plants in Huntington Beach, California, and Toronto, Canada, are installing

DNC systems as well.[39] According to Robert Carlson, manager of manufacturing systems engineering at the division, "DNC is a way of life at McDonnell Aircraft."[40]

Industry sources suggest that NC equipment yields more than one advantage to the firm. Formerly, a machinist had to make individual parts separately. With NC machine tools, someone (either machinist, foreman, or programmer) sets up the machine for a certain part, ascertains that it is working properly, and leaves the repetition to an operator of lesser skill. The result is a diminished need for highly skilled machinists.

In addition, these machine tools leave less scrap than conventional tools. The aircraft industry uses a range of expensive alloys and metals, and therefore the value of this characteristic is substantial. Titanium, for instance, is an essential and extraordinarily costly metal used in aircraft manufacture. By the time critical titanium parts reach the end of the manufacturing phase, they may be worth tens of thousands of dollars each. Therefore, many industry officials place a high premium on the savings NC equipment can yield by minimizing both machining error and scrap.

Besides requiring less blue-collar skill to operate and less metal per part, the new machines are capable of performing more tasks than the old technology. The result is that machine shops are utilizing a smaller number of more sophisticated machine tools. Pratt & Whitney, for example, reduced its ownership of machine tools from 12,000 to 8,000 during the 10-year period ending in 1977, and yet it suffered no drop in overall capacity.[41] P&W has also introduced an IBM 370 computer at its main shop in East Hartford for computer-aided tool selection and the programming of production machines. The same computer is also used for inventory control, thus reducing the costs and time involved in coordinating its geographically dispersed subcontractor network.

Some of the newer raw materials being used by the industry have resulted in a need for still other redesigned machinery. Turbine buckets, for instance, are an integral part of jet engines and are made from a substance that is harder than tool steel. Since this factor presents an obvious problem for conventional machine tools, it has led to the development and use of laser and electrochemical equipment. Pratt & Whitney and General Electric were two pioneers in the use of these techniques. In the airframe sector, similar technological advances are being made. McDonnell Douglas has been experimenting under contract to the National Aeronautics and Space Administration (NASA) with rivetless "glued together" airframes. These experiments hold out the promise of a stronger, smoother aircraft "skin" that eliminates the extraordinarily labor intensive riveting process used in current designs. According to company officials, the potential cost savings are considerable.

To a great extent, the modern capital equipment now available is appropriate only for firms of substantial size. Smaller manufacturers, because of the length of their production runs and their limited financial resources, are less able to incorporate changes in production technology. Because of their size, their workers must be more generally skilled as they usually cannot afford to hire a team of specialized computer programmers for their shop. One Hartford area subcontractor, for example, deliberately steers away from specialized job classifications for precisely this reason. NC tools were available to him long before he brought them into his firm, but he refused to install them before his existing workforce could be trained to program them. Whereas older NC equipment needed highly skilled programmers, the technology of the new machines is such that someone with limited programming experience can become a proficient operator. The owner of this shop was therefore able to introduce NC equipment with little training expense. He maintained that by utilizing this type of technology he was able to "maintain the interest" of his machinists and not lose them to competitors who were "more modern." This particular motivation is probably the exception to the rule. Most firms have introduced the equipment to reduce their dependence on scarce machinist skills.

Summary

As might be expected, all of this technological innovation in the production process has affected the composition of the aircraft industry labor force. Although it is widely agreed by managers that more and more value is being added to the product, the number of production workers relative to non-production employees in the industry has been shrinking for some time. Real value added per production worker in New England's aircraft industry has grown since 1960, despite pro-cyclical variance. In 1960 real value added averaged $17,200 per production worker.

It peaked at $27,000 in 1973, at least $3,000 above its previous high attained in 1969 at the tail end of the Viet-Nam boom.[42] Part of this growth was due to the increased productivity of blue-collar employees, but perhaps a much larger share was due to the value added by non-production engineers, technicians, and programmers. During the 1950s, missile and aircraft products were being perpetually endowed with new technologies, which required a proportionate increase in the number of engineers and technicians. In this transition many job classifications gained importance at the expense of others. The demand for electronic technicians, for example, grew rapidly while the demand for sheet metal workers declined. This situation has, in turn, created a multitude of problems for corporate personnel managers, not to mention the job security problems it poses for labor. It is to this set of issues that we turn in the following chapter.

Endnotes

1. *Iron Age*, October 11, 1976, p. 23.
2. *Ibid*.
3. "P&WA Adding to Test Facilities," *American Metal Market*, September 11, 1978, p. 41.
4. Michael London, "P&WA Buys Maine Plant," *Hartford Courant*, December 26, 1978, p. 1.
5. "Pratt and Whitney Plans to Spend $103 Million to Increase Capacity," *Wall Street Journal*, December 5, 1979, p. 45.
6. *Ibid*.
7. "Why Appalachia," *Industry Week*, December 13, 1971, p. 47.
8. Ray Larsen, "Sikorsky Will Take Helicopter Transmission Output In-House," *American Metal Market*, March 7, 1977, p. 1.
9. *Ibid*.
10. Ray Larsen, "Copter Pact Spurs $100 Million Sikorsky Expansion," *American Metal Market*, March 6, 1978, p. 1.
11. Erwin Bulban, "Backlogs Spurring Helicopter Industry," *Aviation Week*, March 13, 1978, p. 200.
12. "Sikorsky Quits U.S. Coast Guard Contract Bidding," *New England Business*, April 16, 1979, p. 7.
13. "Sikorsky Set to Construct Copter Plant," *American Metal Market*, April 3, 1978, p. 18.
14. Ralph Cordiner, *New Frontiers for Professional Managers* (New York: McGraw-Hill, 1956), p. 56.
15. "GE Board Approves $3 Million Aircraft Engine Plant Expansion," *American Metal Market*, July 2, 1979, p. 17.

16. "GE's Engine Group Will Set Up Airfoils Forge, Cast Plant in Ky.," *American Metal Market*, December 3, 1979, p. 20.
17. Warren Wetmore, "Supplier Strikes Worry Engine Makers," *Aviation Week*, July 23, 1979, p. 23.
18. Michael London, "P&WA Buys Maine Plant," *Hartford Courant*, December 26, 1978, p. 1.
19. Based on data in *Annual Survey of Manufacturers*, Bureau of the Census, U.S. Department of Commerce, 1976.
20. Kay Longcope, "Big Industry in Small Town has Fans, Detractors," *Boston Globe*, January 21, 1979, p. 21.
21. "P&WA Said Lured by Cheap Maine Labor," *Hartford Courant*, December 26, 1978, p. 3.
22. United Technologies 1977 Annual Report, p. 16.
23. United Technologies First Quarter Report, April 10, 1979.
24. United Technologies 1977 Annual Report, p. 3.
25. *Ibid.*, p. 31.
26. Kaman Corporation 1977 Annual Report, p. 4.
27. U.S. Department of Defense, *Departmental Industrial Plant Reserve Report*, approved 9/21/78.
28. "Unit of Boeing to Pay $44.8 Million to GSA for Plant in Wichita," *Wall Street Journal*, December 7, 1979, p. 5.
29. Standard and Poor's, *Industry Survey*, December 31, 1977, p. A29.
30. Charles D. Bright, *The Jet Makers* (Lawrence, Kansas: Regents Press, 1978), p. 13.
31. Merton Peck and Frederic Scherer, *The Weapons Acquisition Process: An Economic Analysis* (Boston: Harvard University Press, 1962), p. 167.
32. *Ibid.*
33. Bright, p. 173.
34. United Technologies 1977 Annual Report, p. 16.
35. "U.S. Lifts Ban on Jet Engine Venture with France's SNECMA," *New York Times*, June 23, 1973, p. 37.
36. Charles Kirby, *Computer Aided Design/Production Equipment*, M.B.A. thesis, Boston College, 1970, p. 6.
37. David F. Noble, "Social Choice in Machine Design: The Case of Automatically-Controlled Machine Tools," MIT mimeo, 1979.
38. Don Yaeger, "McDonnell Douglas Doubles DNC Use," *American Metal Market*, December 12, 1977, p. 12.
39. "McDonnell Douglas Expands DNC Machining," *American Metal Market*, March 12, 1979, p. 12.
40. *Ibid.*
41. "Pratt and Whitney Spends Lavishly to Avoid Machining," *Iron Age*, August 29, 1977, p. 78.
42. Bureau of the Census, U.S. Department of Commerce, *Annual Survey of Manufacturers, 1960–1976*.

Chapter 6

THE AIRCRAFT INDUSTRY
LABOR MARKET

Each new trend in market competition, capital investment, and technology directly affects management strategy and the aircraft industry labor force. From the perspective of management, securing and maintaining a skilled labor force is one of its most difficult assignments. During the contractions that periodically afflict the industry, firms must find ways of reducing employment without permanently sacrificing the best of their skilled workers. During industry booms, employers are forced to scramble for experienced machinists, machine operators, draftsmen, specialized computer programmers, and engineers, all of whom are in scarce supply. Moreover, in the unionized sector, employers must deal responsibly with labor or face the threat of work stoppages that can lead to unfilled orders and conceivably the loss of future business.

From the perspective of the worker, the main concern is finding a comparable job when mass layoffs occur. When Boeing slashed its workforce in the late 1960s in response to collapsing sales, workers generally described it as a catastrophe. Disheartened community leaders displayed bumper stickers that read, "Last One Leaving Seattle Turn Out The Lights!" Despite the boom conditions in the early 1980s, aircraft workers are increasingly alarmed, like their auto worker colleagues, about the growing export of jobs via co-production agreements, joint ventures, and multiple sourcing. Productivity increases are yet another of their concerns. In 1969, for example, it took 25,000 workers to assemble seven Boeing 747s per month, whereas in 1979 the same seven planes were turned out with only 11,000 workers, resulting in far fewer jobs for the unemployed.[1]

These issues, critical to a complete exploration of the industry, are reviewed in this chapter. Special attention is devoted to the New England market because of our limited access to a particularly rich data source, the Social Security Administration's Longitudinal Employer–Employee Data File (LEED). This file allows us to trace a 1-percent sample of all aircraft workers covered by Social Security from 1957 to 1975. Although LEED is a national sample, our access was restricted to data for the six New England states.

Employment Trends in the Aircraft Industry

By this point it should be abundantly clear that aircraft employment is characterized primarily by extraordinarily high variability caused by severe volatility in product demand. This instability is best exemplified by the 35 percent increase in net employment in the brief period between 1964 and 1968, followed by an equally precipitous decline from 1968 to 1972.[2] In less than 48 months, 241,000 workers were added to the industry's employment rolls; in even a shorter period, the same number was let go. In Seattle alone, Boeing reduced its employment by 67,000 in less than three years.[3]

The downturn in employment following peak production for Viet-Nam fell most heavily on the subcontractors, who generally experience much greater fluctuations in employment than the primes. For example, General Electric's Lynn/Everett Aircraft Engine Group experienced a 28 percent increase in employment from 1964 to 1967, followed by a 23 percent decline in the number of production workers during the next eight years.[4] In contrast, during roughly the same period, employment in some Connecticut supplier shops rose by as much as 350 percent only to contract by two thirds between 1968 and 1970.

The ability of prime contractors to bring production in-house during times of decreasing sales is a major reason for this differential volatility. By adjusting the make/buy ratio, prime contractors are in a position to stabilize their own employment levels, in effect, by exporting unemployment to their subcontractors. This "beggar thy neighbor" policy is endemic to the industry and provides the large contractors with a low-cost method of hoarding highly skilled, potentially mobile labor. These fluctuations in employment levels affect the composition of the aircraft labor force in predictable ways. During industry contractions, layoffs, discharges, and forced early retirements by no means fall equally on all groups of workers. Similarly, during expansionary periods, some groups benefit much more than others. As a result, the age, race, and sex composition of the labor force changes over the business cycle.

Demographics of the Aircraft Labor Force

While the proportion of women employed in the industry since World War II has never exceeded 17 percent, a definite employment pattern emerges from the LEED data for New England. Female employment clearly follows a pro-cyclical pattern, increasing with aggregate employment in the industry and falling during recessions (see Figure 6.1). Following the trend in total

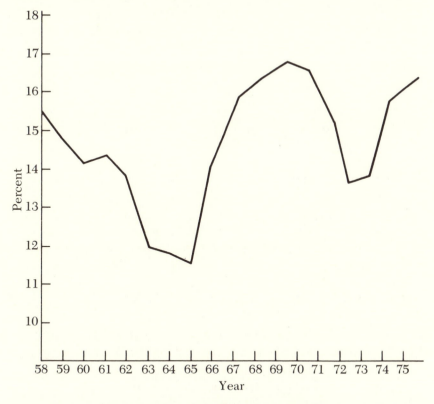

Figure 6.1 Aircraft and Parts (SIC 372) Annual Employment, 1958–1975 — Percentage of Women. (*Source: LEED File Analysis.*)

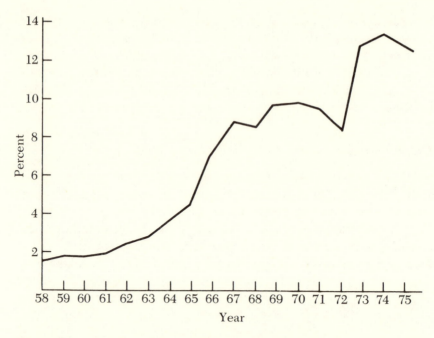

Figure 6.2   Aircraft and Parts (SIC 372) Annual Employment, 1958–1975
— Percentage of Non-Whites. (*Source: LEED File Analysis.*)

industry employment, the proportion of women in the aircraft
sector increased from 11.5 percent in 1965 to 16.9 percent in 1970
before dropping to 13.6 percent in 1972. Although not nearly as
large in magnitude, the pattern is reminiscent of the rise and fall
of "Rosie the Riveter" during World War II.

The pattern for non-white workers is altogether different (see
Figure 6.2). Minority employment in the industry was, by all
appearances, dramatically affected by the passage and implementation of the 1965 Federal Equal Employment Opportunity (EEO)
Act. Its impact is evidenced by the sharp rise in non-white employment as a percentage of the total workforce from 4.2 percent
in 1965 to 7.3 percent a year later. There was another period
between 1972 and 1973 when the proportion of minority employment jumped from 7.6 to 11.5 percent. Most experts concur
that these dramatic increases were due to the industry's heightened sensitivity to EEO regulations given that government contracts require strict compliance with affirmative action.

It seems equally true, however, that the acceleration in minority
hiring was facilitated by the fact that firms were desperate for new

employees in the boom period which happened to coincide with the passage of the EEO legislation. According to the LEED file, more than 39,000 new hires were made by New England aircraft firms in 1966, by far the largest number recorded in that data source. In 1972, 14,000 new workers were hired in a single year, the largest number since 1969. Within this context, it seems appropriate to conclude that the passage and implementation of EEO legislation provided the "incentive" for Defense Department contractors to give greater consideration to minorities, while demand conditions provided the job slots to be filled by minority candidates. It is difficult to determine what would have happened in the absence of the demand boom.

Moreover, it is alleged that some of the compliance with EEO regulations is more apparent than real. At least one large prime contractor in New England has been accused of operating a "revolving door" with respect to minority hiring. Hundreds of minority candidates are cycled through the firm each month, serving all but a few days of the 90-day probationary period. Then, it is charged, the overwhelming majority of these workers are dismissed, often without adequate cause.

The validity of this charge is difficult to assess, particularly because of the nature of the LEED file analysis used to measure the demographic characteristics of the labor force. The level of employment in a given year is based on the number of individuals who worked *anytime* during the year. A group with high turnover, therefore, will tend to show up as having a larger proportion of the total labor force than if the measurement were taken for any single particular day. It follows that if turnover is higher for non-whites, the reported minority proportion of the labor force will be inflated. In an extreme case, the measured growth trend in minority representation in the industry may actually reflect nothing more than excessive turnover, suggesting that the apparent rise in representation is not a sign of labor market success, but one of failure. This measurement is confounded by a wide difference in age between the white and non-white labor force, particularly as younger workers of all races have much higher turnover rates. In 1975 the average age of white men in the New England aircraft industry was 44.5 years; for non-white men it was only 33.2.

Indeed, for other reasons as well, it is the age composition of the industry's workforce that is most intriguing. The pro-cyclical

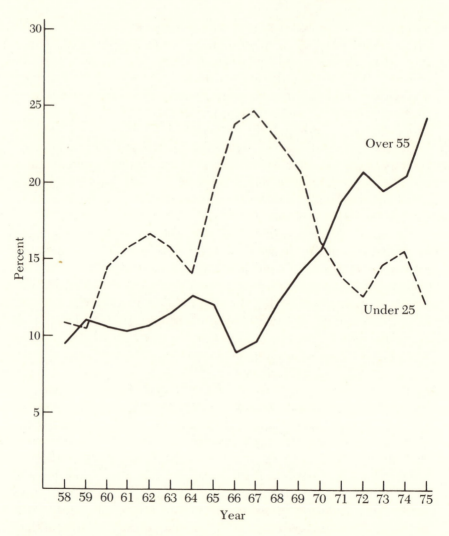

Figure 6.3 Aircraft and Parts (SIC 372) Annual Employment, 1958–1975
— Percentage over Age 55 and Percentage under Age 25. (*Source: LEED File Analysis.*)

pattern identified for women is even more sharply defined among young workers—that is, 25 years of age or younger. Figure 6.3 indicates that employment among this group of workers virtually exploded after 1958, rising from only 10 percent of the total to a full quarter of the workforce in 1966–1967. The industry, which had enrolled mainly prime-age workers (aged 25–54) until this time, exhibited a more youthful appearance on the plant floor and in the administrative offices. Yet, as with women, the end of the

Viet-Nam boom meant that the workers hired last were the first to be let go. Young workers were obviously the last to be hired, and their ranks fell from 25.4 percent of the workforce to only 9 percent. Virtually all of the young workers who were able to obtain new employment were eliminated from aircraft payrolls during this time.

Those remaining, of course, were older workers. With years of seniority and all-around machining skills, both the prime contractors and the suppliers did everything in their power to retain these workers. As a result, workers aged 55 or older, constituting only 1 out of 12 workers in 1966, came to make up a full fifth of the workforce by 1975. In essence the age complexion of the industry had shifted radically. The workers who had been there in the 1950s were, for the most part, spared from permanent displacement while younger workers and women were discharged in massive numbers. The average age of the industry's total workforce increased accordingly from 36.6 years in 1966 to 42.7 in 1975, a 17 percent increase in a 9-year period.

The Age Structure and the Skilled Worker Shortage

The aging of the aircraft labor force may provide a clue to the most frequently voiced complaint in the industry—that in the context of the current boom there is an insufficient supply of skilled aircraft workers. Virtually every firm interviewed in New England agreed that a severe shortage of experienced, blue-collar skilled labor is the most critical problem facing the industry. A similar condition prevails on the West Coast, where Boeing and other airframe manufacturers became so strapped for engineering talent in 1978–1979 that they were forced to enter the European market to secure temporary workers. In its attempt to remain on schedule with the 757 and 767 transport programs, Boeing appealed to other firms in the industry for assistance, renting talent from other companies for which it paid commissions. The company even incorporated appeals for engineering assistance into its requests for proposals from potential 757/767 subcontractors.

Such a critical labor shortage, especially among blue-collar workers, can be understood only in its historical context. During World War II the demand for engineers and machinists was, of course, overwhelming. Under wartime conditions the federal government subsidized general and specific on-the-job training in machine tool skills as a normal part of its military contracts. As in the case of physical plant and equipment, private firms were unwilling to invest in "human capital" that would only contribute to excess capacity in a postwar environment. Workers who were trained were generally in their thirties or older since younger men were subject to the draft. Those trained during the war provided more than an adequate supply of skilled labor during the 1950s and 1960s as the industry shrank to a fraction of its wartime capacity. Even during the Viet-Nam expansion it was possible for both prime and subcontractors to draw on this World War II vintage labor force to supply sufficient skilled workers without costly investment in private training.

The end of the war also brought a dramatic shift in educational resources from vocational training to the sciences and liberal arts. In essence, the government trained a blue-collar labor force through World War II defense contracts and then paid for the training of white-collar workers through the GI bill. Moreover, after a brief stint at retraining skilled workers under the Area Redevelopment Act of 1961, the federal government shifted the focus of manpower programs to providing basic skills to disadvantaged workers, rather than advanced skills to experienced workers who found it necessary to enter new occupations.

Repercussions from these policies were inevitable. The industry's labor force, which had been trained during World War II, began reaching retirement age in the late 1960s and early 1970s. This period was marked by an overall decline in the industry, and therefore, a significant portion of employment reduction was accomplished through normal attrition of these older workers. With the industry's renewed expansion in 1976, however, aircraft firms were left with a diminished supply of skilled workers. In effect, during World War II the government made a massive investment in human capital with a 30-year depreciable life. This capital stock was not seriously augmented during the ensuing period, and consequently in the mid-1970s much of the total stock disappeared almost overnight.

Occupational Structure in Aircraft

The industry's labor problem can be fully understood only in terms of the skill demands in this sector. Table 6.1 lists the occupations

Table 6.1   Occupational Profile of the Aircraft and Parts Industry (SIC 372), 1970

Occupation	Percentage of Industry Employment	Major Occupational Group
Assemblers	6.70	Operative
Engineers, Aero-Astronautic	5.91	Professional, Technical and Kindred workers
Machinists & Appr.	5.86	Crafts
Checkers, Examiners, Etc., Mfg.	5.64	Operative
Other Managers, Administrators	5.32	Managers
Aircraft Mechanics	4.37	Crafts
Secretaries, Other	3.44	Clerical
Blue Collar Worker, Supvr., N.E.C.	3.35	Crafts
Welders, Flame Cutters	3.20	Operative
Engineers, Mechanical	2.36	Professional, Technical and Kindred workers
Expeditors, Production Controller	2.09	Clerical
Drafters	2.04	Professional, Technical and Kindred workers
Tool & Diemakers & Appr.	1.92	Crafts
Misc. Machine Operatives	1.81	Operative
Sheet Metal Workers & Appr.	1.73	Crafts
Engineering, Science Tech., N.E.C.	1.67	Professional, Technical and Kindred workers
Grinding Machine Operatives	1.60	Operative
Accountants	1.58	Professional, Technical and Kindred workers
Engineers, Electrical	1.50	Professional, Technical and Kindred workers
Engineers, Industrial	1.46	Professional, Technical and Kindred workers
Heavy Equip. Mech., incl. Diesel	1.39	Crafts
Other Precision Mach. Operators	1.17	Operative
Operatives, Systems Research	1.05	Professional, Technical and Kindred workers
Store Clerks, Storekeepers	1.05	Clerical

SOURCE: U.S. Bureau of the Census, *Census of Occupations*, 1970.

Table 6.2   U.S. Average Hourly Earnings, 1978 (non-supervisory employees)

	Industry	AHE
SIC 351	Engines and Turbines	$ 8.00
SIC 372	Aircraft and Parts	7.54
SIC 354	Metalworking Machinery	7.02
SIC 369	Miscellaneous Electrical Equipment	6.95
SIC 356	General Industrial Machinery	6.75
SIC 359	Miscellaneous Machinery	6.51
SIC 355	Special Industry Machinery	6.40

SOURCE: Bureau of Labor Statistics, *Employment and Earnings*, March 1979.

in aircraft accounting for 1 percent or more of the industry's total employment. Prominent among these jobs are machinists, mechanics, blue-collar supervisors, welders, tool and die makers, sheet metal workers, and heavy equipment mechanics. These seven craft occupations alone contain more than one in five jobs in the industry. Applying this ratio to the 651,000 aircraft jobs listed in SIC 372 in 1980 suggests that the industry employed more than 140,000 such craftsmen. An additional 12 percent of the workforce is comprised of trained machine operators. Consequently, skilled blue-collar workers make up one third of the industry's total labor force. Given that another 45 percent of the labor force consists of white-collar non-production workers, only about one fifth of all jobs in the industry can be filled by semi-skilled and unskilled blue-collar employees.

Interindustry competition for skilled workers contributes to the shortage in the aircraft industry. Machinists, for example, are used extensively in the metalworking machinery, special and general industrial machinery, electrical industrial, hardware, and engine and turbine industries, as well as in at least 35 other manufacturing sectors. Average wages in these industries in 1978 varied from $6.40 to $8.00 an hour, with aircraft near the top end of the wage distribution (see Table 6.2).

The high average wage might guarantee aircraft firms a steady supply of newly trained employees, if it were not for the fact that skilled workers also consider their long-term employment security when choosing between firms. The volatile aircraft industry simply cannot make a strong case on this issue to potential recruits.

Possible Causes of the Skill Shortage

Knowing the source of the current labor shortage explains why recruitment was troublesome when the industry began to expand again in 1977, but it does not explain why firms apparently failed to take corrective action early enough to avoid it. Training a replacement labor force is a time-consuming process and therefore requires extensive advance planning. The accepted apprenticeship period for a machinist is 4 years, and even the training period for a machine operator can range from 6 to 12 months.[5] Thus, if the industry had begun a massive training program in 1976–1977 when the present expansion first became evident, a shortage of skilled machinists would have persisted to at least 1980 or 1981, well into the expansion cycle.

Industry sources respond that even a perfect forecast of industry demand would not have assured a sufficient labor supply because of the sizeable investment expense entailed in apprenticeship and the uncertainty of the long-run return. In order to be approved by the U.S. Bureau of Apprenticeship and Training (BAT) at the federal level or by a state agency, an apprenticeship program must define the processes to be learned and the number of hours to be spent on each process. A not atypical program for apprentice machinists entails 7,744 hours of shop instruction in 16 different areas and 576 hours of in-class schooling.[6] Each apprentice works four days per week with a journeyman in the shop and spends the fifth day in class. Estimates of the total cost of this training range up to $12,500 per year per employee depending on the occupation.

Individual firms, especially the smaller subcontractors, are reluctant to invest in general machinist training because of the threat of active or passive pirating. By its very nature, "general training" is transferable to firms other than the firm providing it. If the aircraft labor market were perfectly competitive, no firm could afford to offer training at its own expense, because once trained, the worker could choose alternative employment and the original firm would lose its entire investment. Consequently, at least in theory, rational firms in competitive labor markets will provide general training only if the trainees bear the cost by accepting wages lower than those they can receive elsewhere, or if the government assumes the expense.

Indeed, when interviewed, many subcontractors complained of their inability to prevent prime contractors from "raiding" their workforces through the simple incentive of higher wages and greater job security. In periods of a severe labor shortage, employers said that they could not be assured that other local concerns or even national firms would refrain from attempting to lure away trained workers through higher wages or other inducements. As a result, the subcontractors at least are extremely leery of offering general training.

In addition to the threat of piracy, the unwillingness to invest in training is exacerbated by the product demand volatility in the industry. As in the case of machinery and equipment, experience suggests that additional investment undertaken by the industry during boom periods will likely lead to unused capacity two or three years hence. In this case, the firm is often faced with the prospect of not being able to recoup the cost of its investment. The same logic holds true for the individual worker. Paying for one's own general training by accepting a lower wage than available elsewhere is reasonable only if the investment can be recouped after training through steady employment at higher wages. The history of the aircraft industry does not warrant young workers placing a high probability on this occurring.

A serious complicating factor, according to industry managers, is a shortage of readily "trainable" unskilled workers, despite high unemployment among new labor force entrants and especially minorities in the communities where aircraft plants are located. The lack of basic skills alleged by many plant managers is summed up in the complaint of one industrial relations director, who was quoted in the *American Machinist Journal* as saying, "There are some people who come through [our employment office] and I guarantee you they can't convert ½ into a decimal. And these are people who will have to be trained to work to millionths of an inch."[7]

The situation around Hartford, Connecticut, is illustrative. The reported ratio of registered job seekers to job openings was more than 6 to 1 in December 1978[8] with the unemployment rate in the city's black and Hispanic community running at more than 50 percent. Prime contractors in the area, by their own admission, do not perceive this unemployed workforce as "ready" for skill training and philosophically question whether it is the proper role of the employer to offer remedial education in math and English.

For their own part, community spokesmen, including those from the minority community, concur with the skill assessment of the companies, but they claim that it is the social responsibility of local prime contractors to provide remedial training where the public schools have failed. Most argue that it would take longer for the companies to train unskilled minorities because of their math deficiencies, but that it could be done if the companies were willing. A few community leaders hint at racism as a cause of the companies' unwillingness, but the true motivation is likely to be much more complex.

What is abundantly clear is that a severe mismatch exists between the short-run demand for skilled workers and the supply of *already* trained craftsmen and journeymen. Apprenticeship programs, and perhaps remedial education programs to ready workers for apprenticeship, were needed in the early 1970s to provide for the current industry expansion. Neither the industry nor the government met the challenge. The only major observable response has been the industry's attempt to circumvent the skill shortage by relying on more sophisticated capital equipment and altering the occupational structure of production.

Trends in the Aircraft Occupational Structure

One indication of this strategy can be found in the apparent diminishing role of blue-collar workers in the overall production process. While the ratio of production employees to total aircraft employment clearly varies cyclically as shown in Figure 6.4, it also exhibits a downward sloping secular trend, especially among New England's jet engine manufacturers. Expansion in the industry is marked by heavy recruiting of blue-collar production workers, while periods of decline see the same workers subject to widespread layoffs, dismissals, or non-replacement of normal attrition. Engineers, technicians, and administrators are hired in smaller proportions during the boom, but their ranks suffer less during periods of decline. The one exception to this rule is among experienced skilled machinists who are in such short supply that individual firms are extremely reluctant to lay them off temporarily for fear of losing them permanently.

As a result of these employment dynamics, the proportion of production workers in the New England segment of the industry fell from 64 percent in the expansion year of 1966 to a low of 55

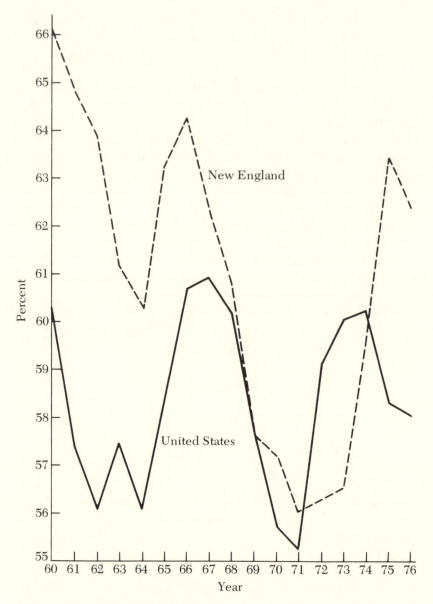

Figure 6.4   Ratio of Production Workers to All Employees, United States and New England, 1960–1976. (*Source: U.S. Bureau of the Census*, Census of Manufacturers, 1960–1976.)

percent in 1971, at the end of the dizzying decline in overall employment.[9] Fluctuations in the U.S. ratio were only about half this magnitude, suggesting that the airframe sector of the industry either subjects its non-production workers to the same kind of employment roller coaster as its blue-collar workforce or it tends to hoard production workers during temporary declines in demand. The former explanation seems more plausible, particularly in light of the large-scale layoffs at firms like Boeing, McDonnell Douglas, and Lockheed beginning in the late 1960s.

The cyclically volatile occupation distribution masks the underlying secular trend only slightly. When a comparison is made of two years with similar levels of value added, a general decline in production workers can be easily detected. For example, in 1961 and 1972, real value added in the New England segment of the industry was roughly equivalent ($856 million versus $869 million), but production workers made up only 57 percent of the total labor force in the latter year whereas they represented 64 percent in 1961. Nationwide the trend was similar but the magnitude was smaller: a difference of only 1.7 percentage points. When other similar two-year comparisons are made, the same results are obtained.

The industry, and particularly the engine-producing sector, has therefore experienced a significant shift from the utilization of blue-collar workers to a greater reliance on overhead employees. The increasing use of computerized numerical control equipment directly contributes to this shift as non-production white-collar computer programmers are substituted for blue-collar machine operators. The technical sophistication of modern aircraft suggests the need for a wider range of technical skills in the industry at the same time that new production methods, including automatic riveting equipment (and soon the rivetless airframe), reduce the need for semi-skilled assemblers and similarly trained workers. This trend has obvious implications for the entire American labor force, not only for the aircraft industry.

Mobility of the Aircraft Labor Force

As one might imagine, the cyclical volatility ever present in the industry ensures an enormous degree of labor mobility into and out of this sector. How firms recruit a labor force during periodic booms and what workers do when they are dismissed during market contractions are critical to understanding the industry's internal operations.

Adjustments in the size of the industry's labor force can be studied in terms of worker tenure and mobility. In this regard, the LEED file for New England is invaluable, for it provides the longitudinal data required to trace specific groups of workers over a significantly long period of time. Using LEED, net employee turnover can be decomposed into gross separations (layoffs, retirements, quits, and dismissals) and gross accessions (new hires and rehires). This process alone allows us to learn a good deal about the industry's labor market dynamics and employee tenure. The LEED file, in fact, permits us to go a step further in that it provides information on the jobs and locations of aircraft workers *before* they enter the industry, as well as *after* they leave it, if and when they do. Thus the "origins" and "destinations" of the aircraft workforce can be traced in detail.

Turnover and Tenure

As Table 6.3 reveals, the separation rate varied from 10.4 to 22.1 percent over the period 1958 through 1975. On average, nearly one fifth of the New England aircraft industry's workforce left the industry each year with as many as 30,600 separations in a single year. What is most intriguing, in addition to the sheer volume, is that during periods of net employment loss, the average separation rate (18.6 percent) was only 3.8 percentage points higher than the rate during employment expansions (14.8 percent). These figures suggest that a large number of the long-term separations, even during fairly severe contractions, may be accomplished through normal attrition rather than forced layoffs.

The accession rate was much more variable during this time, ranging from a low of 1.8 percent during the 1970–1971 "crash" to a high of 37.9 percent in 1965–1966. It averages over 22 percent in net growth years, but less than half this rate during periods of net decline. The relative stability of separations, in contrast to the fluctuating accession rate, clearly implies that the industry, except in the very short run, adjusts its employment level by varying its hiring rate. Normal turnover is so high that, excluding periods of total collapse, firms must continually hire new workers simply for replacement. This situation was exacerbated by the surge of retirements in the late 1960s.

Table 6.3 Separation and Accession Rates in the New England Aircraft Industry, 1958–1975

Turnover Year	Gross Separations	Separation Rate	Gross Accessions	Accession Rate	Net Δ
1958–1959	18,900	20.5%	11,600	12.6%	−7,300
1959–1960	11,000	14.0	19,400	22.8	8,400
1960–1961	14,000	15.0	15,900	17.9	1,900
1961–1962	13,900	14.6	16,600	16.4	2,700
1962–1963	15,300	15.6	12,200	12.4	−3,100
1963–1964	12,200	12.8	12,400	13.0	200
1964–1965	14,000	14.7	24,100	25.3	10,100
1965–1966	20,100	19.1	39,900	37.9	19,800
1966–1967	22,600	18.1	36,200	28.9	13,600
1967–1968	30,600	22.1	23,800	18.0	−6,800
1968–1969	28,000	21.2	20,500	15.5	−7,500
1969–1970	26,800	21.5	10,200	8.2	−16,600
1970–1971	21,800	20.2	1,900	1.8	−19,900
1971–1972	16,700	19.9	7,300	9.3	−9,400
1972–1973	8,200	10.4	14,800	18.9	6,600
1973–1974	13,000	15.3	12,000	14.1	−1,000
1974–1975	10,000	11.9	4,600	5.5	−5,400
$\bar{X}$	17,418	16.8%	16,612	16.3%	
SD	6,642	4.2	10,105	11.3	
SD/$\bar{X}$	.381	.242	.608	.638	

SOURCE: LEED File Analysis.

These numbers support the contention of prime contractors that their companies have not permanently laid off large numbers of workers in recent years. The reduction in employment from 22,000 production workers to 9,200 by one prime contractor between 1968 and 1971 involved only 2,000 permanent layoffs according to company/union records. Most actual permanent layoffs have occurred within the subcontractor network, which in New England comprises less than one fifth of all reported aircraft employment.

None of this implies that there have not been widespread layoffs of a short-term nature. Virtually all prime contractors as well as the suppliers are known for using temporary layoffs to adjust production levels when work is scarce. These adjustments are usually accomplished after overtime hours have been reduced, and often after the imposition of short work weeks. The temporary layoffs, which affect primarily blue-collar production workers, can range from a matter of a few days to six months or more.

While temporary job losses normally do not pose a major crisis for the workers involved, they cannot be categorized as trivial.

According to survey research, they often involve serious strains on family resources in the short run and in some cases produce long-lasting anxiety about future security. This type of job loss has its own set of financial, emotional, and even physical consequences that are of real concern to the aircraft worker.

The Sources of New Hires and the Destinations of Former Aircraft Workers

To personnel managers labor problems are most acute during periodic booms, not recessions, for they are the ones charged with the responsibility of recruiting new workers in enormous numbers. For example, between 1964 and 1967, the industry in New England required over 100,000 new workers to replace those leaving the industry and to provide an additional 43,000 workers to the net employment stock.

The 1967 aircraft labor force of 138,700, according to LEED, included 71,000 workers who were not working in the industry as late as 1964 (see Table 6.4). Of these workers, 900 or 1.3 percent of the new accessions were hired from aircraft firms located in other regions of the country with an additional 9,000

Table 6.4   Origin of New England Aircraft Employees (Destination: 1967)

	% of Total (Total = 138,700)	% of Accessions (Total = 71,000)
Origin—1964:		
Origin in SIC 372—In Region	48.8	—
Origin in SIC 372—Outside Region	.7	1.3
NICE*	10.5	20.6
Military/Reserves	6.1	11.9
"Primary" Sector	19.6	38.5
"Secondary" Sector	14.3	27.7
(Origin outside region)	(6.4)	(12.7)
Top 5 Industries:		
SIC 35 Machinery, excl. Electrical	2.7	5.2
SIC 54 Food Stores	2.0	3.8
SIC 36 Electrical Equipment	1.8	3.5
SIC 50 Wholesale Trade	1.6	3.1
SIC 38 Instruments	1.4	2.7

SOURCE: LEED File Analysis.
* NICE = "not in covered employment."

recruited from outside New England where they had been working in other industries. Thus nearly 14 percent of the new recruits were from outside the region, with the vast majority of these workers having no aircraft industry experience.

From within the region, over one fifth (20.6 percent) of the additions to the employment rolls came from outside the covered labor force. Presumably most of these workers were not working before they joined an aircraft firm, although some had previously been in federal government work or other employment not covered by Social Security. Another one in nine workers (11.9 percent) found employment in the industry when they left the military. Virtually all of them were young men.

The vast bulk of the workforce (66.2 percent), however, was recruited from other industries with the majority coming from other "primary" sector employers. The primary sector is defined here to include all durable manufacturing industries as well as the extraction industries, construction, the higher skilled service sector (for example, banking, real estate, and insurance), and government service. Actually, 1 in 20 of the new workers came from the closely allied metal-working machinery industry, while others entered from presumably similar jobs in the electrical equipment and instrument-producing sectors. To what extent these workers were "pirated" through special inducements, besides the promise of higher earnings, cannot be ascertained. What is obvious, however, is that at least during the Viet-Nam-induced boom, the industry was capable of luring workers away from other sectors of the economy. Most of them came from other durable manufacturing jobs, a large proportion having experience and skills. Women apparently gained the most from these aircraft openings, for they transferred into this more lucrative industry from the generally lower-wage retail sector and from other "secondary" employers in the health services and non-durable manufacturing industries.

During the subsequent collapse of the industry, workers apparently moved back to the same regions and types of industries from which they originally came. Between 1967 and 1972, 77,800 or 56 percent of the 1967 workforce left or was forced to leave aircraft firms in New England. Table 6.5 traces this group of workers to their 1972 destinations. Only 2 percent remained in the industry by relocating to firms in other parts of the country. Another 9.5 percent retired (or left as a result of disability or

Table 6.5   Destination of New England Aircraft Employees (Origin: 1967)

	% of Total (Total = 138,700)	% of Separations (Total = 77,800)
Destination—1972:		
Remain in SIC 372—In Region	43.9	—
Remain in SIC 372—Out of Region	1.2	2.1
NICE	9.4	16.7
Retired, Disabled, Deceased	5.3	9.5
Military/Reserves	1.3	2.3
Unknown	.7	1.3
"Primary" Sector	29.9	53.3
"Secondary" Sector	8.3	14.8
Top 5 Industries:		
SIC 35 Machinery, excl. Electrical	5.2	8.6
SIC 50 Wholesale Trade	3.0	4.9
SIC 90 Government	2.3	3.8
SIC 36 Electrical Equipment	2.2	3.7
SIC 34 Fabricated Metal	2.1	3.4

SOURCE: LEED File Analysis.

death), and nearly 17 percent left the covered workforce altogether. The remaining 68 percent found employment in other
sectors, with over half (53.3 percent) locating in other "primary"
industries. One in seven was working in a "secondary" sector job
in 1972. As we noted above, many of the women who entered
the industry between 1964 and 1967 came out of the health services sector in large numbers. During the postwar period, many
returned to it.

A comparison of the top five industries in the origin and destination studies suggests that workers move back and forth among
the same limited number of industries. This, no doubt, is related
to occupational similarities, but it suggests that if the business
cycles of the key durable manufacturing industries were to become
more synchronized, workers and firms would likely be faced with
severe adjustment problems. The decline in aircraft employment
preceded the general economic recession of 1971, and therefore
a large number of workers were able to find jobs in non-aircraft
sectors. If the general recession had coincided precisely with the
downturn in aircraft, many more skilled workers would have faced
the prospect of long-term unemployment.

As it was, the workers most adversely affected by the aircraft
industry decline of 1967 to 1976, at least in New England, were

not aircraft workers themselves. Rather it appears from the turn-over and destination studies that those most disadvantaged by this sustained industry downturn were younger workers and others wishing to enter the industry who never received the opportunity to be hired into the industry in the first place. Together with the high turnover of youth in the labor market, this explains the steady erosion in the proportion of young workers in the industry noted earlier in this chapter. These young workers appear to bear the brunt of the industry's long periods of decline, acting as the labor buffer in this volatile market.

Wages and Earnings in the Aircraft Industry

The prospect of substantially better compensation in the aircraft industry is clearly the key factor in the industry's past ability to recruit workers during aircraft booms. Because of the skill com-position of the workforce, the average wage in the industry com-pares favorably to most sectors of the U.S. economy. In 1978 production workers earned $7.54 an hour, 22 percent more than the average manufacturing wage and a third more than average earnings in the overall private sector.[10]

Nonetheless, wages in some manufacturing industries exceed aircraft by a considerable margin and appear to be rising faster. Chief among these industries are motor vehicles, cement, blast furnace products, and primary non-ferrous metals (see Table 6.6). As late as 1967, average earnings in the auto industry were only

Table 6.6   U.S. Average Hourly Earnings of Selected 3-Digit Industries, 1978

Industry	Average Hourly Earnings	Percentage above Aircraft and Parts
SIC 331 Blast Furnace Products	$9.41	24.8
SIC 324 Cement, Hydraulic	8.63	14.5
SIC 333 Primary Non-ferrous Metals	8.56	13.5
SIC 371 Motor Vehicles and Equipment	8.51	12.9
SIC 341 Metal Cans	8.04	6.6
SIC 374 Railroad Equipment	8.02	6.4
SIC 351 Engines and Turbines	8.00	6.1
SIC 321 Flat Glass	7.94	5.3
SIC 372 Aircraft and Parts	7.54	—

SOURCE: Bureau of Labor Statistics, *Employment and Earnings*, March 1979.

2.9 percent greater than in aircraft; by 1978 the differential had
widened to 12.9 percent. The gap has widened even more in
other industries. The differential between basic steel and aircraft
increased from 3.5 to 24.8 percent over the same period. Part of
the difference may be due to relative union strength, reflecting
the weaker position of organized labor in aircraft.

Domestic aircraft workers are also paid somewhat less than their
European counterparts. Manufacturing wage rates in Belgium,
West Germany, Canada, Holland, and Sweden are now higher
than the national average in the United States (see Table 6.7).
This is one reason why industry sources maintain that production
is more costly in Europe. In addition, although wages are lower
at this time in Japan, France, Britain, and Italy, the gap between
these countries and the United States is narrowing as wages rise
more rapidly in these nations.

The fact that labor costs are higher abroad, specifically in the
aircraft industry, is nearly universally accepted. The industry's
leading journal, *Aviation Week*, drew special attention to this issue
in discussing the F-16 NATO co-production agreement. *Aviation
Week* pointed out,[11]

> *The problem of higher production costs in Europe has been gaining
> increasing attention in recent months, and the F-16 situation is
> further underscoring the problem. Production man-hour costs in
> Western Europe's aerospace industry appear to range anywhere*

Table 6.7   Compensation per Hour in 10 Countries: All Manufacturing
Industries

| Nation | Compensation per hour | | | | 1960–1974 Annual Rate of Gain |
	1960	1970	1974	Mid-1975	
United States	$2.66	$4.20	$5.65	$6.07	3.4%
Canada	2.12	3.46	5.49	6.10	4.1
Japan	0.26	0.99	2.70	3.00	10.2
France	0.81	1.75	3.41	4.65	5.9
Germany	0.83	2.32	5.25	6.27	5.8
Italy	0.63	1.75	3.43	4.55	6.3
Britain	0.82	1.48	2.51	3.34	4.0
Belgium	0.82	2.05	5.18	6.74	6.5
Holland	0.64	1.99	4.91	6.19	7.5
Sweden	1.20	2.93	5.48	6.93	7.1

SOURCE: International Association of Machinists (IAM).

from 20–50% higher than those of U.S. companies, taking European social security benefits into account. On top of this, productivity in many European firms is only about half that of U.S. companies.

An interview with one of New England's jet turbine manufacturers confirmed the higher production costs in Europe. The company maintains that building one of its large turbines overseas costs 30 percent more than producing it in New England.

The cost advantage of American aircraft production is also not unknown to Europeans, as evidenced by an address before the Belgian parliament in 1976 by Minister of Defense Paul Van Den Boeynants. He bemoaned the fact that, "American hourly wages are lower than hourly wages in Belgium, inflation is under better control in America than in Europe, American productivity is higher than ours, and the American technological capacity is also superior to ours."[12] Although aircraft employers may find other problems with it, the U.S. workforce has definitely not priced itself out of the market.

Labor, Output, and Productivity

This last conclusion is reinforced by the fact that real productivity growth in the industry has greatly exceeded increases in the level of total payroll costs since at least 1960. Despite the fact that productivity, as measured by real value added per production worker hour, ceased to grow after 1972, paralleling the experience in other industries, it has continued to eclipse real payroll gains as shown in Table 6.8. Productivity peaked at $14.11 in 1972, but the ratio of value added to total payroll costs continued to increase from 1.40 in 1960 to 1.73 in 1972 to 1.91 in 1976. Over the entire period, productivity in real terms increased by 65.1 percent, or 3.2 percent annually.

Productivity gains, however, have not been uniform across the industry as Table 6.9 indicates. Despite the high capital investment rate noted in the previous chapter, productivity advances in the engine-producing New England region have lagged behind those in the United States as a whole. Real value added per production worker hour was virtually identical in New England and the United States in 1960. During the next 17 years real productivity in the region rose by 35 percent compared with the national rate of 65 percent. This figure translates into an annual

Table 6.8　Productivity Growth in the U.S. Aircraft Industry, 1960–1976

	1960	1964	1965	1968	1969	1972	1975	1976	1960–1976
Value Added/ Production Worker Hour (real dollar)	$8.34	$11.04	$11.27	$11.91	$12.83	$14.11	$13.18	$13.77	+65.1%
Value Added/ Total Payroll	1.40	1.50	1.55	1.65	1.63	1.73	1.94	1.91	+36.4%

SOURCE: U.S. Bureau of the Census, *Annual Survey of Manufacturers, 1960–1976.*

Table 6.9　Real Value Added/Production Person-Hour in the United States and New England, 1960–1976

	1960	1964	1965	1968	1969	1972	1975	1976	1960–1976
New England	$ 8.31	$ 9.17	$ 9.89	$11.13	$12.00	$11.75	$10.76	$11.25	+35.4%
United States	8.34	11.04	11.27	11.91	12.83	14.11	13.18	13.77	+65.1%
Ratio (NE/US)	1.00	.83	.88	.94	.94	.83	.82	.82	

SOURCE: U.S. Bureau of the Census, *Annual Survey of Manufacturers, 1960–1976.*

improvement rate of 1.9 percent in New England, only three fifths of the national average. This rate was despite the fact that real dollar capital expenditures per worker were normally larger in New England than in the United States as a whole (see Table 6.10), and despite the fact that as a percentage of total aircraft industry investment, New England's share rose from 11 percent in 1960 to more than 15 percent during the mid-1970s.[13]

In light of these capital expenditure data, the relatively slower growth in New England's productivity cannot easily be explained. One possibility is that the newly installed plant and equipment in New England is simply not as productive as the new fixed capital used in the airframe sector. Engine production continues to utilize a large proportion of skilled machinists, while airframe uses a much larger number of semi-skilled assemblers. It is conceivable that advances in the assembly process have overshadowed any gains in the more labor-intensive machine trades.

An alternative hypothesis—based on the higher blue-collar skill composition in engine production—suggests that the New England lag is due to greater labor hoarding in light of the severe shortage of machinists and other skilled metal workers. By this reasoning, New England firms retain more of their labor during industry downturns, preferring to take a temporary loss in productivity and profit rather than a permanent loss in skilled workers.

Indeed, a comparison of value added and total payroll in the United States and New England provides clear evidence of substantial hoarding by the engine producers. During the expan-

Table 6.10   Capital Expenditures per Worker in the Aircraft Industry, United States and New England, 1960–1976

Real Capital Expenditures per Employee (1967 = 100)							
1960	*1964*	*1965*	*1968*	*1969*	*1972*	*1975*	*1976*
N.E. $380	$450	$790	$800	$780	$350	$600	$710
U.S. 290	440	520	750	810	320	520	610

Real Capital Expenditures per Production Worker (1967 = 100)							
1960	*1964*	*1965*	*1968*	*1969*	*1972*	*1975*	*1976*
N.E. $570	$750	$1,250	$1,310	$1,340	$630	$950	$1,130
U.S. 480	780	880	1,240	1,400	540	890	1,050

SOURCE: U.S. Bureau of the Census, *Annual Survey of Manufacturers*, 1960–1976.

Table 6.11   Growth in Value Added and Total Payroll, U.S. and New England Aircraft and Parts Industry, 1960–1976 (based on current dollars)

	1960–1964	1964–1967	1967–1971	1971–1976	1960–1976
United States:					
%Δ Value Added	18.9%	44.8%	−13.4%	29.9%	93.6%
%Δ Payroll	13.1	38.1	−20.0	15.6	44.4
New England:					
%Δ Value Added	17.0%	65.7%	−36.6%	57.8%	93.9%
%Δ Payroll	29.0	51.1	− 7.6	10.2	98.5

SOURCE: U.S. Bureau of the Census, *Annual Survey of Manufacturers*, 1960–1976.

sionary periods of 1960–1964, 1964–1967, and 1971–1976, the proportional change in value added among all aircraft firms in the United States exceeded the proportional change in total payroll (see Table 6.11). This was also true of New England in the latter two periods. During the steep contraction of 1967 to 1971, however, the decline in payroll exceeded the decline in value added in the United States. This was in sharp contrast to New England's experience in which payroll costs were cut by only 7.6 percent versus a collapse of 36.6 percent in value added. This could only have occurred if the jet engine producers had retained their skilled labor in the face of declining sales. It also suggests that layoffs cut much more deeply into the airframe market than the engine market. The fact that during the 1971–1976 recovery value added rose almost six times faster than payroll in New England provides additional evidence that the productivity differences between this region and the United States stem from different labor policies. These policies are partly related to technology, but also reflect the historical legacy of the skilled worker shortage.

Sources of Employment Loss in the Aircraft Industry

The degree of labor hoarding and the apparent difference in labor policy between airframe and engine producers can be further illuminated by determining quantitatively which factors have been most responsible for the changes in employment levels in the industry. This can be done by using data from the *Annual Survey of Manufacturers* to decompose total employment change over any discrete period of time into the amount due to (1) reduction in value added, (2) changes in productivity, and (3) changes in average hours worked by the production labor force. Mathematically, this is accomplished by taking the total discrete differential of the following identity:*

$$PW \equiv VA \cdot \frac{MH}{VA} \cdot \frac{PW}{MH}$$

where

$$PW = \text{number of production workers}$$
$$VA = \text{value added in real terms}$$
$$MH = \text{production person-hours}$$

As an example, we can apply the methodology to the period 1965 to 1976. The total value of New England aircraft shipments in real terms was nearly identical at \$1.55 billion in the years 1965 and 1976. Yet the number of production workers at the end of the period was 7,200 or 17.4 percent smaller than at the beginning. Part of this decrease can be explained by the fact that real value added in the region declined by 20 percent over the period as more intermediate production occurred among subcontractors, licensees, and joint venture partners outside the region. As a consequence the ratio of value added to value of shipments

---

* The total discrete differential of this identity has the following form:

$$dPW \equiv \underbrace{\left(\frac{MH}{VA} \cdot \frac{PW}{MH} \right) dVA}_{\text{due to } \Delta \ VA} + \underbrace{\left(VA \cdot \frac{PW}{MH} \right) d\frac{MH}{VA}}_{\text{due to } \Delta \ \text{productivity}}$$

$$+ \underbrace{\left(VA \cdot \frac{MH}{VA} \right) d\frac{PW}{MH}}_{\text{due to } \Delta \ \text{person-hours/worker}}$$

$$\underbrace{+ \left(VA \cdot d\frac{MH}{VA} d\frac{PW}{MH} \right) + \left(\frac{MH}{VA} \cdot dVA \, d\frac{PW}{MH} \right) + \left(\frac{PW}{MH} \cdot dVA \, d\frac{MH}{VA} \right)}{}$$

$$+ \left(dVA \, d\frac{MH}{VA} d\frac{PW}{MH} \right)$$

$$\underbrace{}_{\text{interaction terms}}$$

fell from 57.5 to 46 percent. Over the same period, productivity (real value added per production worker hour) rose by 13.8 percent, increasing from $9.89 to $11.25.

	Summary of Data (all dollar figures in real terms)		
	1965	1976	%Δ
Value of Shipments	$ 1,550 m	$ 1,550 m	0%
Value Added	$ 892 m	$ 713 m	− 20.1
Production Workers	41,500	34,300	− 17.4
Hours Worked	90.2 m	63.4 m	− 29.7
Value Added/Value Shipments	.575	.460	− 20.1
Value Added/Person-Hour	$ 9.89	$ 11.25	+ 13.8
Hours/Production Worker	2,173	1,848	− 15.0

When we substitute these figures into the algorithm for the discrete differential, we find the following results:

Total Net Employment Loss	− 7,200
Change due to:	
1. Reduction in New England Value Added	− 8,327
2. Increase in Productivity	− 5,007
3. Reduction in Annual Hours/Worker	+ 7,299
4. Interaction Terms	− 1,165

The single most important factor responsible for the net loss in aircraft jobs in New England was the movement of production outside the region. This is by no means a surprising result, confirming the importance of the competitive factors mentioned in Chapter 4. This single phenomenon is responsible for a gross loss of jobs exceeding the total net loss.

Productivity increases were responsible for the elimination of an additional 5,000 jobs in the jet engine sector, some of which occurred as the result of greater reliance on numerical control equipment as a partial substitute for skilled blue-collar labor. The "interaction" between factors (for example, the increase in productivity as a response to a reduction in hours worked) accounted for the remaining gross loss of 1,165 jobs.

If there had been no offsetting factors, the total decline in employment would have been 14,500, an elimination of fully *one third* of the 1965 workforce. As it was, the displacement in New

England was substantially tempered by another form of labor hoarding—a cutback on average hours worked so that workers in effect shared the unemployment. The average work week was cut from 41.8 to 35.5 hours to accomplish a gross "gain" in employment of nearly 7,300.

Over the same period, the decline in total U.S. aircraft employment was handled in a very different way. Nationwide the industry underwent a decline in the value of shipments and even greater losses in value added and net employment. Value added declined by 26 percent from $8.8 to $6.5 billion. The number of production workers plunged by nearly 37 percent, compared with 17 percent in New England.

In this case, however, a reduction in average annual hours per production worker accounted for only a gross "gain" of 18,000 jobs against a net loss of 137,700 in employment. Along with the "interaction effects," this factor could offset only a tiny fraction of the 98,000 jobs lost because of reduced value added and the 68,000 jobs lost as a result of productivity advances.

Total Net Employment Loss	− 137,700
Change due to:	
1. Reduction in U.S. Value Added	− 98,291
2. Increase in Productivity	− 68,018
3. Reduction in Annual Hours/Worker	+ 17,854
4. Interaction Terms	+ 10,755

Thus, here again, New England engine manufacturers handled the industry contraction in a very different manner from their counterparts in the airframe market. The nature of technology and the size of the labor pool very likely induced the two segments of the industry to behave as they did in the labor market.

Unionization in the Aircraft Industry

The way that aircraft firms operate in the employment market is also colored by the existence of trade unions in the industry. The International Association of Machinists (IAM) represents more aircraft workers than any other union. Its coverage includes Boeing, General Dynamics, Lockheed, McDonnell Douglas, and United Technologies among the largest primes as well as Beech Aircraft, Cessna, Gates Learjet, and Piper Aircraft among the smaller general aviation firms. The United Automobile Workers Union (UAW), actually the United Automobile, Aerospace, and Agricultural Implement Workers of America, represents workers in several McDonnell Douglas facilities as well as Martin Marietta and North American Rockwell. The International Union of Electrical Workers (IUE) represents aircraft workers through its contracts with the General Electric Aircraft Engine Group. Ironically, even the Carpenter's Union is well represented in the industry, a legacy from the days of Hughes Aircraft's "Spruce Goose."

Various differences between subcontractors and primes have been noted in previous chapters. One further distinction involves the extent of employee unionization. Generally, the subcontractors are unorganized. One of the reasons involves the historical volatility in industry employment. Since the suppliers experience an even greater degree of instability within their labor force, unions have found it difficult to organize the smaller shops. In addition, some of the smaller firms employ a large number of immigrant tool and die workers and machinists who are generally unreceptive to the U.S. labor movement. Union attempts to organize the smaller vendors have also been thwarted in some cases by younger workers more interested in "cashing out" their total compensation than in gaining added fringe benefits such as improved pension plans. Since some vendors can afford to pay comparable wages by offering fewer fringe benefits, younger workers are often reticent to change the *status quo* and therefore find no reason for joining a union.

As a rule, organized labor in aircraft is weaker than in autos, steel, rubber or electrical equipment—comparable manufacturing industries. Part of the reason for this appears to be related to historical factors, whereas some of it may be related to the organizing effort made by the unions in this industry. In the Northeast, for example, Grumman Aircraft on Long Island, New York, has remained union free since its establishment while Pratt & Whitney has perennially succeeded in denying union shop privileges to the IAM. In terms of wage advances, aircraft workers gained wage parity with their counterparts in auto and steel during the 1960s, but have since lost ground.

Work Stoppages

Despite signs of union weakness, the prime contractors in aircraft have been subject to numerous strikes as has been the case in other major manufacturing industries. According to U.S. Department of Labor statistics, there were over 600 strikes against aircraft and parts manufacturers between 1927 and 1959.[14] As a result, over 8 million person-days of production were lost, mostly in the West Coast airframe market.

Since 1960, however, there have been a number of major and a bevy of minor strikes against the jet engine manufacturers. GE, for example, has been the target of several IUE strikes over the past 15 years, including lengthy strikes in 1966 and again in 1969 when the entire national GE system comprising 233 plants in 33 states was shut down by the 13 unions that represent workers at the company.

The response of GE—as well as an increasing number of other producers—is to use labor strategies aimed at insulating their production from disruption. There is strong evidence, for example, that GE's moves to Rutland, Vermont, in the early 1960s and to Madisonville, Kentucky, in 1980 were to escape unionization. Some union officials also believe that Pratt & Whitney's move to North Berwick, Maine, was motivated primarily by a similar strategy.

The rapidly spreading use of multiple sourcing by the primes may also be related to unionization and union-led work stoppages. Strikes in 1979 at two key suppliers forced slowdowns in the delivery of F100 engines by Pratt & Whitney. The strikes were long enough to induce the engine producer to seek out other sources of supply and to commit $57 million in investment funds to the expansion of its North Berwick facility. With the growing competition among primes focused on on-time delivery, these strategies designed to circumvent union strength will very likely be implemented by a larger array of producers. Co-production and joint venture agreements already serve this purpose.

Trade Unions on the Defense

By far the most urgent issue facing aircraft unions is that posed by the growing internationalization of the industry. Besides resulting in drastic cutbacks in employment, the global expansion has served to further destabilize organized labor. The unions' response has been to seek government aid for their affected members. The IAM has requested that the U.S. Department of Labor determine their members eligible for Trade Readjustment Assistance (TRA) as a result of the transfer of work overseas. The adjustment assistance, if granted under the Trade Act of 1974, would make workers eligible for training, job search, and relocation allowances, as well as TRA payments equal to 70 percent of previous weekly earnings for a period of as much as a full year.

According to union leaders, this type of aid, while necessary, merely treats the symptoms and does not directly deal with the problem of "runaway jobs." To meet this challenge, union representatives have argued that corporate tax laws need to be rewritten and collective bargaining agreements need to be improved. In this regard the IAM has called for curtailment of overseas tax deferrals, repeal of the foreign tax credit, and contract language that restricts subcontracting out of the bargaining unit.

The degree to which the new union drive to protect their members' jobs will be successful is as yet unknown. With the current boom in the industry, union demands are to some extent being relegated to a back burner. When the boom ends, however, it is very likely that a renewed attempt at circumscribing the power of aircraft firms to cut jobs and move investment to non-union areas will be undertaken by organized labor. What happens then will be part of an as yet uncharted future history of labor–management relations.

Summary

The trends outlined in this chapter suggest that the current improved prospects for the industry will not be shared equally by corporate stockholders and labor. The trend in the value added/value of shipments ratio can be expected to continue downward with more production work being transferred to new parallel facilities, multiple sources, and foreign producers. The reason will not be because American aircraft workers are pricing themselves out of the market, but rather because of the exigencies of international competition and the intentions of prime contractors to insure themselves against potential disruptions of production. The role of labor in the aircraft industry therefore merits close examination during the course of the current industry expansion and what will inevitably be, if history provides any indication at all, the industry's subsequent contraction.

Endnotes

1. "Masters of the Air," *Time*, April 7, 1980, p. 54.
2. U.S. Bureau of the Census, *County Business Patterns*, 1959–1977.
3. *Time*, April 7, 1980, p. 54.
4. Figures provided by District 2, International Union of Electrical Workers (IUE), Lynn, Massachusetts.
5. U.S. Congress, House Subcommittee on Special Investigations of Small Business Problems of the Select Committee on Small Business, *Problems of the Tool and Die Industry and Associated Problems of Manufacturers and Distributors of Machine Tools:* Hearings on H. Res. 13, 89th Congress, 2nd Session, July 26–27, 1966, p. 85, in Glynnis Trainer, *The Metalworking Machinery Industry*, Joint Center for Urban Studies Harvard–MIT, 1979, p. 87.
6. Susan Qualtrough and Joseph Jablonowski, "Filling the Need for Skilled Workers," Special Report 712, *American Machinist*, June 1979, p. 137.
7. *Ibid.*, p. 136.
8. Office of Community Development and Planning, City of Hartford, "Comprehensive Economic Development Strategies," May 1979, p. 23.
9. U.S. Bureau of the Census, *Annual Survey of Manufacturers, 1960–1976*.
10. Bureau of Labor Statistics, *Employment and Earnings*, March 1979.
11. Robert Ropelewski, "NATO Consortium Expects Satisfactory F-16 Offset," *Aviation Week*, February 23, 1976, p. 17.
12. *Ibid.*, p. 18.
13. Calculated from U.S. Bureau of the Census, *Annual Survey of Manufacturers, 1960–1976*.
14. U.S. Department of Labor, Bureau of Labor Statistics, Division of Wages and Industrial Relations, "Work Stoppages: Aircraft and Parts Industry, 1927–1959," p. 3.

Chapter 7

RELATIONS WITH GOVERNMENT

Ultimately, all observations about trends in the aircraft industry lead back to its relations with the federal government. Long before the United States had a policy on school desegregation or social security, it had a policy on the aircraft industry. With few exceptions, that policy has been to encourage the industry's health and prosperity through direct purchases and often outright subsidy. In the domestic arena aircraft has enjoyed the equivalent of most favored nation status.

The industry has matured to the point where it has reduced its dependence on its traditional benefactor. No longer does the federal government buy as much of the industry's product, nor does the government control the industry's behavior as it once did. Still, the government plays a major role in maintaining industry prosperity, despite its gradual relinquishing of direct intervention and sponsorship.

"Shelters" and Support

One instructive way to analyze any economic entity's relations with government is to rely on the concept of "shelters." A shelter· is any market entry barrier provided by some level of government that insulates an industry or firms within it from normal competitive pressures. Government shelters may take many forms. One example is the enforcement of copyright and patent laws. Another is the conferring of monopoly status, as in the case of a public utility.

The aircraft industry benefits from a wide array of shelters that have been cultivated over the years. The major shelters can be placed into three categories: research and development funding, government-subsidized plant and equipment, and contracting procedures. All have been mentioned in previous sections of this book, but now we will examine them more closely.

Federal Research and Development Funding

The aerospace industry performs over 20 percent of all industrial research and development in the United States.[1] The most obvious characteristic of this R&D effort is that the federal government supports so much of it. Indeed, R&D contracts account for a major portion of the industry's revenue. In this sense, the government is almost a guarantor of continued product improvement.

Table 7.1 reveals the importance of R&D investment for the

Table 7.1   Aerospace Industry R&D Funds as a Percentage of Gross Revenues (in millions of 1967 dollars)*

Year	R&D Funds	Percentage of Total Sales
1960	$3,687	20.3
1961	4,039	21.3
1962	4,263	21.1
1963	4,975	23.4
1964	5,334	24.6
1965	5,340	24.9
1966	5,610	22.4
1967	5,669	20.8
1968	5,635	19.9
1969	5,574	22.6
1970	4,768	21.0
1971	4,304	22.2
1972	4,234	21.9
1973	4,038	20.5
1974	3,457	20.1
1975	3,330	20.1
1976	3,351	20.4
1977	3,641	21.3
1978	3,749	20.3
1960–1978 mean	4,474	21.5

SOURCE: Aerospace Industries Association, *Aerospace Facts and Figures 1980–81*.
* Adjusted by the Producer Price Index for all Industrial Commodities.

Table 7.2 Aerospace Industry R&D Effort by Source of Funds, All
Industries and the Aerospace Industry (in millions of 1967
dollars)*

Year	Total R&D for All Industries	Total Aerospace	Aero. % of Total	Govt. Funded	Privately Funded	% Privately Financed
1960	$11,027	$3,687	33.4%	$3,305	$381	10.3%
1961	11,506	4,039	35.1	3,626	413	10.2
1962	12,092	4,263	35.2	3,784	478	11.2
1963	13,336	4,975	37.3	4,499	477	9.5
1964	14,193	5,334	37.6	4,853	480	8.9
1965	14,714	5,340	36.3	4,667	673	12.6
1966	15,784	5,610	35.5	4,795	814	14.5
1967	16,385	5,669	34.6	4,531	1,138	20.0
1968	17,003	5,635	33.1	4,433	1,201	21.3
1969	17,271	5,574	32.3	4,296	1,278	22.9
1970	16,420	4,768	29.0	3,665	1,102	23.1
1971	16,048	4,304	26.8	3,418	886	20.5
1972	16,440	4,234	25.7	3,429	804	18.9
1973	16,617	4,038	24.3	3,173	864	21.4
1974	14,563	3,457	23.7	2,691	765	22.1
1975	14,050	3,330	23.7	2,585	744	22.3
1976	14,593	3,351	23.0	2,589	762	22.7
1977	15,340	3,641	23.7	2,840	801	22.0
1978	15,950	3,749	23.5	2,842	907	24.2

SOURCE: Aerospace Industries Association, *Aerospace Facts and Figures 1980/81*.
* Adjusted by the Producer Price Index for all Industrial Commodities.

industry. Historically, such expenditures have equaled one fifth
of total industry sales and were close to one fourth immediately
preceding the Viet-Nam escalation. Table 7.2 indicates that the
lion's share of industry R&D has come from the U.S. government.

In addition, Table 7.2 discloses two significant trends that began
in the mid-1960s. In 1964 the aerospace industry's share of the
nation's total R&D effort was at its peak, 37.6 percent, while the
industry's own dollar contribution to this work was at its ebb, 8.9
percent of the total. Considered together, the two facts imply that
government subsidization of aerospace was then at its maximum.
Since that time, the publicly financed share of the total has declined, and the amount of R&D financed by the companies themselves has increased.

These data suggest a causal relationship between diminishing
government support of R&D and the rise of international joint
ventures. Multinational development of aircraft products first became common in the late 1960s, or shortly after the government

began to reduce its funding of aircraft R&D. It seems plausible that firms, barred from acquiring requisite amounts of development capital from the federal government, would seek it overseas. This has been one of the major reasons offered by industry representatives for the growth of joint ventures. As the reader will recall from Chapter 5, under the terms of the GE/SNECMA agreement to develop the CFM56 turbine, the French government contributed 50 percent of the $500 million required for research and development. International capital has therefore been substituted for domestic public support.

Research and development funds provided in military prime contract awards are distributed among the regions generally in proportion to total sales or payroll. Approximately 39 percent of these funds, amounting to a total of $8.5 billion in 1979, went to firms on the West Coast, with 13 percent allocated to New England and another 13 percent to the South Atlantic states (see Table 7.3). Over 88 percent of all these funds went to business firms, with the rest about equally divided between educational institutions and other non-profit organizations.

This distribution varies widely among regions. New England's educational and private non-profit research institutions together garner more R&D support than those of any other region, including the Pacific. This fact is consistent with the area's high-technology base, and the fact that the more technologically sophisticated aerospace products (MIRVs, helicopters, and jet turbines) are made there. The government-university-aerospace complex is obviously one of the more critical reasons why the advanced technology end of the industry has remained, and indeed expanded, in New England. On the other hand, most R&D on the West Coast is handled outside the universities in the airframe plants themselves. In both cases the industry benefits from nearly $9 billion in tax-supported research.

Federally Owned Plant and Equipment

Government-sponsored R&D, of course, is only one shelter provided to the industry. Direct provision of physical capital and government contracting policy add to the overall degree of market insulation. In this way the aircraft industry's relations with the federal government are almost unique. At the outbreak of World War II, it became evident that the industry's plant space would

Table 7.3 Military Prime Contract Awards of $10,000 or More for Research, Development, Testing and Evaluation (by region and types of contractor, FY 1979, in millions of dollars)

Region	Total		Type of Contractor					
			Educational Institutions		Other Non-Profit Institutions*		Business Firms	
	$	%	$	%	$	%	$	%
New England	$1,087	12.9%	$139	24.2%	$158	37.8%	$789	10.6%
Middle Atlantic	849	10.0	51	8.9	13	3.1	785	10.5
East North Central	387	4.6	34	5.9	21	5.0	333	4.5
West North Central	930	11.0	4	.7	1	.2	925	12.4
South Atlantic	1,128	13.3	203	35.4	48	11.5	876	11.8
East South Central	192	2.3	3	.5	4	1.0	185	2.5
West South Central	340	4.0	21	3.7	6	1.4	313	4.2
Mountain	305	3.6	48	8.4	1	.2	257	3.4
Pacific†	3,236	38.8	71	12.4	166	39.7	2,999	40.2
Total	$8,454	100.0%	$574	100.0%	$418	100.0%	$7,462	100.0%

SOURCES: Department of Defense, "Military Prime Contract Awards by Region and State" (annual), and Aerospace Industries Association, *Aerospace Facts and Figures 1980/81*.
* Includes contracts with other government agencies.
† Includes Alaska and Hawaii.

have to be expanded radically. As we noted previously, individual companies refused to finance this expansion themselves, fearing that war contracts would not endure as long as the normal capital amortization period. The government, resolved to increase aircraft output, overcame the industry's reluctance through a variety of economic concessions. One of the first concessions was a special, temporary depreciation allowance that provided incentives for privately financed construction. Firms were allowed to depreciate newly constructed plant space over the course of 5 years for tax purposes, as compared to the normal 20-, 30-, or even 40-year period.

But by itself this allowance proved an insufficient incentive in persuading firms to make the massive capital investments necessary to meet the production quotas set by President Roosevelt. Consequently, the federal government turned to the actual construction of war plants, which were leased to the aircraft companies for production after being built by the Army Corps of Engineers. After the war, contracts were canceled by the score, and the government was left with acres of idle plant capacity and two practical alternatives: continue leasing the plants or sell them to the aircraft firms outright.

Unable to encourage most aircraft manufacturers to purchase the plants after the war, the government continued to supply the industry with fully equipped plants until 1957.[2] In that year the government altered its policy on aircraft production facilities and since then has made a more concerted effort to induce firms to purchase leased sites in order to reduce the implicit subsidy offered the industry. Nevertheless, neither the Air Force nor the Navy has met with any great success in this endeavor, for firms naturally prefer to keep plant space a variable rather than a fixed cost and gain the additional advantage of paying no local property tax on their plant. They therefore retain their lease arrangements when and where possible.

Data on the extent of direct government investment in the industry are scarce and generally unreliable, mostly because of the government's negligent record keeping. In the early 1970s, however, the Assistant Secretary for Installations and Logistics of the Department of Defense reported that the number of government-owned plants had been reduced from 288 in 1954 to 189 in 1972.[3] It is not known which companies use which government plants, but one source, Robert J. Gordon of Northwestern University, has arrived at some industry-wide figures. He notes,[4]

> *The aircraft industry, in particular, is a virtual ward of the government, having contributed approximately 10 percent of the funds for its own expansion in World War II and only about one third during the Korean War. . . .*

Although much of the machinery supplied during those two wars is now fully depreciated or obsolete, a large number of the plants are still in operation. Some no longer manufacture aircraft products, but there are still many remaining that do. Again, according to Gordon,[5]

> *Much of the aircraft and ordnance production for the Vietnam War has been carried out by private firms with government-owned plant and equipment. . . .*

This provision is clearly an advantage for the aircraft industry, one that few other industries share. It adds significantly to the rate of return on private assets, allowing firms a sizeable profit on a small capital base.

Contracting Procedures

The aircraft industry also operates under a variety of favorable contractual arrangements with the government. Owing to the fact that unforeseen technical difficulties may arise in the development phase of a product, accurate estimation of cost in advance of production is often difficult. Ostensibly for this reason, cost-plus contracts have been the rule in the industry. Years ago the "cost-plus-percentage-profit" contract was common. Under this arrangement, firms were paid a predetermined percentage of total costs as a profit. This type of agreement naturally gave firms an incentive to keep costs as high as possible once they were awarded a contract, and it was therefore discontinued.

The "cost-plus-percentage-profit" was replaced by the "cost-plus-fixed-fee" contract. Under this method, suppliers are paid a fixed, absolute profit, regardless of the level of final costs. This contract has become the most prevalent type of agreement, although during Robert McNamara's tenure as defense secretary, many of the production contracts were changed to the conventional total fixed price variety. McNamara established a new kind of contract based on the Total Package Procurement Concept (TPPC). This system required contractors to incorporate the entire development and production cost of an aircraft or missile in their original bids. In the mid-1960s, when inflation began to accelerate, cost overruns became rampant, forcing manufacturers to absorb increased costs. Industry leaders complained bitterly, and the cost-plus-fixed-fee contract was reinstated, again giving producers a guaranteed profit.

This type of contract is an obvious shelter that may or may not be justified. The intent behind it is to protect firms from unexpected costs that often are incurred while experimenting with new technology. Although this type of agreement originated in a period of stable prices, it has become an important shield against double-digit inflation. Unfortunately for the taxpayer, it also shields the industry from many of its own mistakes, inefficiencies, and waste.

Government Purchasing Policy

Support of R&D, federal leasing arrangements, and cost-plus contracting are three special shelters the government has provided for the aircraft industry, but these alone do not encompass the full range of relations between the state and this particular sector of the "private" market. Even with the accelerated growth in the commercial and general aviation segments, as well as the export boom, the U.S. government historically has purchased over half of total industry output. The historical "stop-go" pattern of government purchases has therefore been the dominant force behind the industry's cyclical instability.

Since 1967 the government's importance as a customer has diminished. During the Viet-Nam War almost two thirds of total aircraft, engine, and parts sales went to the federal government (see Table 7.4). Following the end of hostilities, defense purchases fell below 50 percent and remained there with the exception of 1976 and 1977. Then in 1979 the proportion dropped precipitously as a result of an explosion in commercial sales and stable current dollar expenditures by the government. What will happen to the ratio in the 1980s cannot be known, of course. Commercial sales will likely continue to expand, but the Reagan administration's expected boost in aircraft procurement may offset this expansion, pushing the ratio back up to 50 percent or more. Even so, few

Table 7.4 Aircraft, Engine, and Parts Sales, by Customer, 1966–1979 (in millions of current dollars)

Year	Total	U.S. Government	Other	% of Total Sales to U.S. Government
1966	$8,725	$5,458	$3,267	62.6%
1967	11,894	7,141	4,753	60.0
1968	13,850	7,411	6,439	53.5
1969	12,764	7,161	5,603	56.1
1970	13,466	7,586	5,880	56.3
1971	11,392	6,313	5,079	55.4
1972	10,153	4,954	5,199	48.8
1973	12,278	5,539	6,739	45.1
1974	13,542	5,982	7,560	44.2
1975	14,656	6,859	7,797	46.8
1976	15,936	8,314	7,622	52.2
1977	16,378	8,848	7,530	54.0
1978	19,305	8,724	10,581	45.2
1979	$24,501	$8,868	$15,633	36.2%
1966–1979 Mean Percentage				51.2%

SOURCE: Aerospace Industries Association, *Aerospace Facts and Figures 1980/81*.

experts expect that the federal government will ever again dominate the market as it did before the 1970s.

The significance of this trend should not be underestimated. As the government has reduced its purchases and R&D funding, the industry has been forced to seek new sources of financing outside the United States. Although joint ventures might still have been pursued in the absence of declining federal support, it is apparent that the reduction gave greater urgency to this type of foreign market penetration. Again the multinationalization of the industry can, at least partially, be traced to changes in government policy toward the industry.

Federal Regulation

Federal handouts are not without cost. Although the U.S. government assists the aircraft industry with various types of financial aid, it also subjects the industry to many forms of regulation. Direct regulation of the industry is not significantly different from that of other manufacturing industries, but aircraft's preeminent size makes it extremely important. Not all relevant regulation, however, is direct. Regulation of the airlines, the largest class of end users excluding the government, has a major impact on manufacturers.

Direct federal regulation comes from a variety of federal agencies, including the Federal Aviation Administration (FAA), the Environmental Protection Agency (EPA), the Occupational Safety and Health Administration (OSHA), and American Metals Standards (AMS). Industry representatives invariably describe the regulations issued by these agencies as a nuisance. All officials interviewed complained about the paperwork costs involved; one small subcontractor with sales of $6 million per year estimated his regulatory compliance costs to be $20,000 annually. No single firm reported that its competitive stance was hurt by compliance costs, however. They reasoned that since all producers were forced to comply, no single firm was hurt.

One individual offered some insightful thoughts on direct federal regulation. He foresaw a day when compliance costs would hurt American producers as a class; if foreign manufacturers continue to improve their competitive standing, he said, this cost advantage could easily be parlayed into a price advantage. The same individual, however, strongly believed that regulations have some advantages. He maintained that compliance costs "keep fly-by-night, shoestring operators out of the marketplace." In other words, regulation itself has a sheltering aspect.

Some federal regulations have even been known to affect the market demand for the industry's product beneficially. Two recent government edicts, for example, have in large part been responsible for the current boom in aircraft: EPA emissions and noise standards, and deregulation of the airlines by the Civil Aeronautics Board (CAB).

The stringent new EPA standards have made older jet turbines obsolete. As we noted in an earlier chapter, airlines will be required to either retrofit the older planes in their fleets with a new generation of quieter and more fuel-efficient engines, or ground them altogether. This factor alone played a major role in the unprecedented surge in aircraft orders in 1979.

The recent deregulation of the airline industry is having a similarly beneficial impact upon equipment manufacturers. Open price competition and even outright fare wars among airlines soon after deregulation increased the demand for airline seats, ultimately creating a derived demand for aircraft and parts. During the busy travel seasons of 1978 and 1979, airlines reaped enormous profits from the surge in traffic. The increased demand was clearly a result of lower prices, which allowed more people than ever to travel by air. The net change in passenger miles flown because of deregulation, however, will depend in the future on the airlines' ability to exploit an elastic demand schedule for passenger travel. In the economically uncertain 1980s, this may prove to be a formidable task.

As many of the rural and commuter routes once serviced by the major carriers are transferred to the smaller commuter airlines, a new generation of efficient mid-size aircraft will be required for this market segment. This requirement will lead to the development and production of new airframes and engines, stimulating additional growth in the aircraft sector. The FAA is now allowing a capacity of 58 seats for the commuter lines, up from the previous 19 seats. By altering this regulation, the FAA has provided a catalyst for the more rapid development of the commuter airline industry, and in the process it is creating new growth markets for the aircraft industry itself. In this case a small change in a government regulation is responsible for spawning an entire new industry segment.

Relations with Foreign Governments

Government relations and regulations do not stop at the U.S. border. In the world market for aircraft the vast majority of commercial exports are made to foreign governments rather than private sector airlines, for most foreign commercial airlines are, in fact, state-owned national carriers. The balance of export sales are made to foreign military establishments. Thus, another level of government directly affects the industry, adding new political factors to the already highly politicized industry.

Aircraft purchases often manifest the economic policy of the respective state. It is the official policy of several Western European governments as well as the Japanese government that national enterprises acquire advanced technologies in order to develop internationally competitive industries. Moreover, in determining from whom to buy, competitive factors such as price and quality are not nearly as important as job creation and trade balance. The recent competition between Pratt & Whitney and

General Electric to provide Air France, a nationalized carrier, with commercial power plants, has already been mentioned in this regard.

Military exports, of course, are even more politically sensitive than exports in the commercial sector. Sales depend upon U.S. foreign policy, trends in U.S. political dominance, and the stability of foreign governments sympathetic to the United States. The political situation in Iran is illustrative of this point. Aerospace contractors lost billions in potential sales when the Khomeini government canceled a total of $7 billion in U.S. contracts.

Changing relationships between U.S. government policy and the policies of foreign governments also directly affect aircraft sales. When exporting military products, American manufacturers actually sell to the U.S. government, which then resells the product to the foreign government. Sales of military aircraft products are subject to the review of several government agencies, including the Departments of Defense, State, Commerce, and Justice. In some cases, military exports are subject to congressional review. Congress has been known to link the granting of export licenses to issues like international fishing agreements and foreign human rights policies. Industry leaders have responded by complaining bitterly when political issues such as these are allowed to block what could have been extremely lucrative sales to foreign countries. Although many executives have in fact indicated their concern with the issue of human rights, some have requested that the government issue waivers in some sales when foreign competitors wait in the background to provide products similar to those produced by U.S. firms. Estimates of recent losses by the U.S. aircraft industry because of restrictive government trade policies approach $2.5 billion[6] (see Table 7.5). Here again, price and quality are insignificant factors in the determination of sales, making the aircraft market almost unique in American enterprise. One would indeed have difficulty in explaining the dynamics of the industry in terms of standard cost curves, supply, and demand.

Relations with State and Local Governments

The level of operations in an industry often determines the level of government at which the most significant relations take place. This is probably nowhere more evident than in the aircraft in-

Table 7.5 Blocked U.S. Aerospace Orders Filled by Foreign Competitors

Country	System Purchased	Quantity	$ Millions	U.S. System Denied	Quantity	$ Millions
Kenya	Hawk Trainer (UK)	12	70.2	A-4	12	83.3
South Africa	SS-2 Missile (France)	1800	N.A.	500MD	40	28.0
	Transall C-160 (France)	N.A.	N.A.	C130H	16	170.0
Sudan	Mirage F1 (France)	29	420.5	A-10	29	174.0
	BO.105 (W. Germany)	10	16.9	Bell 206	10	5.0
Taiwan	Shafrir (Israel)	N.A.	N.A.	Maverick	N.A.	N.A.
Philippines	BO.105 (W. Germany)	38	64.1	AH-1	38	138.7
Portugal	Alpha Jet (France)	56	705.6	A-4	56	388.8
Spain	Mirage F1 (France)	48	700.0	F-18	48	768.0
Brazil	Mirage 3 (France)	4	N.A.	A-7	4	27.8
Ecuador	Mirage F1 (France)	58	841.0	A-7	82	703.5
	Jaguar (UK)	12	120.0	Kfir (U.S. engine)	N.A.	N.A.
Honduras	Mystere (France)	12	N.A.	A-6	12	178.3
Peru	Su-22 (USSR)	32	250.0	A-4	32	222.2
Egypt	Swingfire (UK)	2,000	75.0	TOW-G	N.A.	N.A.
	Mirage 2000 (France)	N.A.	N.A.	A-10	N.A.	N.A.
India	Jaguar (UK)	200	2,000	Swedish Viggen (U.S. engine)	200	1388.0
Kuwait	Scorpion (UK)	129	20.0	M113A1	129	12.9
United Arab Emirates	Mirage 2000 (France)	N.A.	N.A.	A-4	N.A.	N.A.
Oman	Jaguar (UK)	12	120.0	A-4	12	83.3
Pakistan	Mirage (France)	32	332.0	A-7	110	700.0
Morocco	Mirage F1 (France)	50	650.0	F-5	N.A.	N.A.
	Alpha Jet (France)	N.A.	N.A.	T-2	N.A.	N.A.
	Agusta Bell (Italy)	6	N.A.	CH-47	6	N.A.
Chile	Bandeirante (Brazil)	N.A.	N.A.	Super King Air 200	N.A.	6.0
Libya	G-222 (Italy)	20	358.0	L-100-30	12	150.6

SOURCE: *Aviation Week and Space Technology*, May 7, 1979. Table compiled by American League for Exports and Security Assistance, Inc., Washington, D.C.

dustry. The major prime contractors in this sector negotiate with high-level officials of national governments in the United States and abroad. Relations with state and local governments are secondary, and the sheer power of the primes often provides them a dominant position in enterprise–local government relations.

State and local governments therefore have very little direct or indirect influence on the larger aircraft manufacturers. Most prime contractors argue that existing sunk costs, skilled labor pools, and proximity to research institutions far outweigh the tax advantages or disadvantages that state and local governments can offer. Many smaller subcontractors express similar opinions in regard to the impact of state fiscal and regulatory policies upon their operations. In interviews, most stated that they would obviously prefer lower taxes and less "red tape," but neither of these factors seriously threatens the viability of firms or encourages them to relocate. Again, the nature of competition in the industry makes price a less critical factor, and thus cost disadvantages become less important.

Nonetheless, state and local governments still attempt to influence location decisions by granting tax abatements and other incentives. Pratt & Whitney's move to North Berwick, Maine, provides one such example. Still it is unlikely that P&W would have chosen another site had the $2.1 million tax abatement not been granted. In the final analysis other factors were simply much more important.

Summary

One is forced to conclude from all of this that without the federal government, there would simply be no aircraft industry, despite the fact that the commercial market is playing a much larger role than it has in the past. No aspect of the industry, including the commercial sector, could exist without the R&D funds provided by the state or the state's purchases of military equipment. It is no accident, then, that virtually every other nation has an aircraft industry that is either heavily subsidized or indeed owned by the state.

But what is perhaps more important for understanding the changing nature of the industry is the changing pattern of government influence. With the decline in federal R&D funds and reduced procurement levels, the industry has not only become less dependent on the public sector, but has had to shift its particular allegiance as well. Foreign governments, by virtue of their ability to control both military and commercial aircraft procurement and the supply of investment capital directly, are increasingly viewed by the industry as a substitute for domestic government aid. As a consequence, aircraft has become the leading multinational industry in the world, and as such there is less and less reason to maintain full production capacity at home. In a sense, then, this industry, even while weighted down by its immense sunk costs, is becoming one of the most agile and "footloose" industries in the nation.

Endnotes

1. Aerospace Industries Association, *Aerospace Facts and Figures 1978/79*.
2. Charles D. Bright, *The Jet Makers* (Lawrence, Kansas: Regents Press, 1979), p. 170.
3. *Ibid.*, p. 171.
4. Robert J. Gordon, "$45 Billion of U.S. Private Investment Has Been Mislaid," *American Economic Review*, June 1969, p. 224.
5. *Ibid.*
6. James Ott, "Industry Leaders Rap U.S. Export Policy," *Aviation Week*, May 7, 1979, p. 19.

Chapter 8

THE AIRCRAFT INDUSTRY: PROSPECTS FOR THE FUTURE

This final chapter is devoted to summarizing our major findings and the corresponding implications for capital expansion and employment in the aircraft industry. Here we focus on the primary characteristics of the industry and the recent trends that have altered the industrial dynamics of this key manufacturing sector. The critical importance of sales volatility, new competitive strategies, and the rapidly growing internationalization of production are reviewed with an emphasis on the consequences for capital financing and the employment prospects for the industry's labor force. We also consider the changing nature of government policy toward the industry and the industry's growing reliance on the civilian sector, for both have altered the dynamics of the industry and affected the viability of individual firms.

We also present in this chapter a series of policy recommendations that are seen by company and trade union representatives as crucial to promoting the industry's prosperity. In highlighting these positions, we hope to raise an awareness of the policies considered necessary for maintaining the industry's competitive position in the world market and for improving the economic security of its workforce.

Finally, in the last section of this chapter, we turn our attention to the future of the industry, focusing on the need for better private and public sector planning to assure the industry's continued growth and security.

Sales Volatility and Market Competition

We have seen that the aircraft industry is one of the nation's most cyclically volatile in terms of sales, profits, and employment. The sector exhibits its own unique business cycle consisting of two components, one for commercial and one for military aircraft. The degree of convergence between the two market cycles determines the overall state of the industry. As shown in Chapter 3, convergence at the present time has sparked a substantial boom in sales and profits. The implications for domestic employment are not quite so sanguine, however, for the reasons discussed in Chapters 4 and 6.

In the latest expansionary phase of the cycle, dominance in the commercial airframe market appears to be attaining a level not experienced since the early 1960s. To replace an aging and largely fuel-inefficient generation of aircraft, it appeared until recently that the traditional airframe rivals, Boeing, McDonnell Douglas, and Lockheed, might all make serious bids for supplying the next generation of commercial aircraft. By the end of 1980, however, Boeing was clearly on its way to reasserting its dominance in this segment of the market. Within the next three to four years it may capture as much as 70 percent of the world's new airfleet. With the exception of the recent European entry, Airbus Industrie, the remaining commercial producers seem unwilling or perhaps financially unable to spend the billions of dollars required to compete directly with Boeing.

Precisely the opposite is happening in the jet engine producing sector. The market for large commercial turbines, at one time completely dominated by Pratt & Whitney, has undergone a radical transformation in the last two decades. The rivalry between P&W, General Electric, and Rolls Royce has reduced the leader's share of the market from 92 percent in 1966 to 63 percent in 1978. At the same time, GE's dominance in the military sphere has been successfully challenged by P&W, particularly as a result of the firm's F100 engine, which powers three of the major U.S. and NATO fighters. As a product of this market interpenetration, the jet engine market has become more intensely competitive despite its oligopolistic character. GE's aggressive pursuit of a substantial share of the commercial market through its CF6 turbine and the jointly produced GE/SNECMA CFM56 is the primary force promoting this trend. Pratt & Whitney's PW2037, introduced as the power plant for Boeing's 757, is P&W's all-out attempt to recoup its losses in this sphere.

Who wins the battle for dominance in the airframe and engine markets will not necessarily affect the fortunes of the industry as a whole, but the nature of the competition has clearly had a serious impact on production and employment levels in specific regions of the country. The specific marketing and production strategies used to secure market share—parallel production, multiple sourcing, co-production, joint ventures, and licensing—have all tended to increase the geographical dispersion of production, affecting the communities that have traditionally been aircraft industry centers. Production facilities have been relocated to overseas markets as well as to new areas in the United States.

The Internationalization of the Industry

Basic industrial reconstruction following World War II largely precluded the development of indigenous aircraft industries in Europe and Japan, and the stage of economic development in other countries made it virtually impossible to assemble the investment funds or technology to do so. As a result, since the war foreign countries have turned to the United States for military and commercial aircraft. American firms have been more than happy to exploit this lucrative market. Given the cyclically volatile nature of domestic demand, the unpredictable nature of Defense Department procurement, and reduced federal government subsidy of research and development, the U.S. industry has even accelerated its pursuit of international sales. It has been extraordinarily successful. Two thirds of all turbine-powered aircraft in service in the world today are of U.S. manufacture. By 1979 aerospace contributed $10.1 billion to the U.S. trade balance, up from $2.8 billion a decade earlier.[1]

The wrinkle in this development involves the nature of competition initiated in response to the growing worldwide market. U.S. aircraft firms have begun to compete for sales on the basis of co-production percentages as well as price and quality. Since virtually all foreign commercial and military sales are made to governments rather than to private firms, overseas purchasers are often willing to pay a premium price in return for a share of production that reduces their import balance and creates employment for their own workers. Over time, increased competition for foreign sales has led to larger concessions on co-production and consequently fewer jobs for U.S. aircraft workers. This in part explains the decline we noted in the value added to value of shipments ratio in New England between 1965 and 1976.

In addition to expanding sales, the international market has provided new sources of capital, but this development has also had its price. The need for sources of R&D funds other than the Defense Department has provided sufficient incentive for U.S. producers to enter into joint venture agreements with foreign, government-owned or -subsidized firms. In return for a share of any profit generated from sales and an infusion of technology, U.S. firms have been able to obtain much of the front-end capital they need for product development and pre-production facilities. Yet as this trend toward internationalization continues to develop, it is likely that the technological advantage U.S. prime contractors currently enjoy will be eroded. Fueling European and Japanese competition may eventually result in fewer sales and substantially less employment.

The Supply Side of the Market

We have seen that the supply side is split between the prime contractors and the subcontractor network. Current trends appear to favor the primes but not necessarily the smaller firms that supply them. The primes have historically been able to weather the aircraft cycle by varying their make/buy ratios at the expense of their suppliers. Now the intensification of competition within the industry has put an additional burden on local subcontractors.

As the demand for guaranteed "on-time delivery" has emerged as a critical factor in successful contract bidding, the primes have sought ways to signal to their potential customers their ability to perform. The multiple-sourcing strategy, which takes a portion of subcontract work out of its traditional locations, is one method used for this purpose. The rise of parallel production facilities is another. "Cost minimization" in the conventional sense does not legitimately apply to these strategies. Companies use them because of the inestimable cost of sales foregone if potential purchasers believe that they are incapable of meeting delivery schedules. Both multiple sourcing and parallel production entail the loss of economies of scale in a technical sense, but given the nature of competition in the industry, price and therefore measured dollar cost is often not the sole or even most relevant criterion in a successful sales strategy. Multiple sourcing minimizes the risk of vendor supply disruption, while parallel production facilities reduce the risk of internal work stoppage. The use of these strategies by prime contractors is not overlooked by potential customers.

Advances in transportation and communication technology have drastically reduced the economic costs of shipping parts and co-ordinating production activities, thereby permitting the utilization of these production strategies. In effect, the agglomeration economies that once favored local subcontractors are now outweighed by agglomeration diseconomies. In connection with the imperatives of co-production and joint ventures, we expect that the various local vendor markets will not fully recover from the losses endured in the post–Viet-Nam period. It is in this segment of the market that sales and employment losses will likely be permanent.

Capital

The most striking trend in the aircraft industry has been the shift to foreign sources of capital for research and development. As product development costs have skyrocketed, making R&D programs "bet your company" propositions, the primes have sought ways to augment retained earnings and federal government funds with investment resources from foreign governments and public and private multinational consortia. Foreign sources who are financially strong, but technologically weak, are willing partners in joint ventures, especially if there are benefits with respect to trade balance, domestic employment, and technology transfer.

Although the prime contractors have alternative avenues and strategies for securing investment funds, the vendors are not as fortunate. Given their size they normally are unable to enter into international agreements. Moreover, they generally find it difficult to secure venture capital from domestic sources. Because of the highly volatile nature of the industry and the consequent high mortality rate, commercial banks and other institutional lenders are often unwilling to risk long-term debt on vendors. As a recourse, the subcontractor is often forced to seek an acquisition bid by a larger firm in order to secure necessary capital.

Just as the banks are unwilling to finance small firms operating in such a volatile industry, larger aerospace concerns have recognized that too much dependence on aircraft production alone is a highly risky proposition. As a result, some firms have begun the process of economic conversion, while others have pursued strategies of diversification through conglomerate merger.

As we noted in Chapter 5, one of the most striking examples of conversion involved the Kaman Corporation of Bloomfield, Connecticut. Before 1965 Kaman was a producer of sophisticated military helicopters, but given the competition from the much larger Sikorsky and Bell operations, the firm found itself too susceptible to market vagaries. Management was ingenious in successfully converting its production facilities and labor force to the manufacture of acoustic guitars, windmills for electric power generation, and other non-aerospace products. Unfortunately, Kaman seems to be the exception to the rule. Attempts by Grumman and Boeing to use their aerospace know-how for the production of mass transit vehicles have proven less than successful.

The most notable case of diversification can be found in the acquisition activities of United Technologies Corporation, parent to Pratt & Whitney, Hamilton-Standard, and Sikorsky. Its acquisition of Otis Elevator, Carrier Air Conditioning, the Essex Group, and AMBAC/American Bosch over the past five years has reduced the corporation's reliance on the federal government to less than 30 percent of its gross sales.

While both conversion and diversification can potentially be beneficial in terms of profitability, the type of conversion undertaken by Kaman appears to be much more beneficial for existing communities and local employment than the diversification strategy followed by UTC. This is true because conversion usually entails the maintenance of physical plant and employment in the original community, while diversification through merger will often entail no new employment opportunity or capital investment in existing facilities. Of the 109 individual production facilities acquired by UTC since 1970, only one was located in New England, the home base of the parent corporation. This type of diversification may be useful in insuring stockholders against risk, but it does little to improve the economic security of the workers or communities in the existing aircraft-dominated regions.

Labor

Although the industry is in the midst of a sales boom and a partial resurgence in labor demand, the overall long-term employment picture for aircraft workers is somewhat cloudy. Several trends are evident.

Superimposed upon the cyclical upswing in labor demand is a severe shortage of skilled, experienced labor. In the case of machinists, the dearth of current supply can be traced to the retirement of many workers who were trained during World War II and who provided a surplus of blue-collar skills through the mid-1970s. The postwar shift in educational resources away from vocational training exacerbated the overall condition. The supply and demand for skilled workers appears to be an exceptionally good example of the "cobweb" phenomenon in which supply and demand are never perfectly equilibrated because of long lag times and uncertainty in the market adjustment mechanism.

The skilled worker shortage has been one of the factors contributing to the rapid introduction of computerized machine tools, and indirectly puts additional pressure on firms to pursue multiple sourcing and parallel production. Over the long run, the shortage may be ameliorated by the substitution of technicians for skilled blue-collar workers, the greater utilization of computerized tools, and the export of production as a consequence of co-production and joint venture activity. During a period of buoyant demand this poses no problem for labor, but the end of the current boom will likely leave a much larger number unemployed as a result of these factors.

A sad commentary on the current situation is that while jobs go begging for a lack of experienced, blue-collar, skilled workers, unemployment rates among youth and minorities in the areas closest to existing plants are abnormally high. In few industries is "structural" unemployment—a persistent mismatch between job vacancies and unemployed workers—so evident. Neither the public schools nor the vocational education systems seem to have adequately prepared the unemployed for skilled work in the industry. For whatever reasons, firms were extremely tardy in bring-ing the problem to national attention.

Relations with Government

The degree of market "sheltering" and government support for the aircraft industry is nearly unique in the American economy. Perhaps only shipbuilding compares in the extent to which the industry relies on government sales and subsidies for survival. Nearly half of all aircraft sales are still made to the U.S. govern-ment, although the percentage has declined from well above 60 percent during the Viet-Nam era.

This special relationship has been promoted by three factors:

(1) the government's ability to dominate the market through the sheer volume of its purchases;
(2) Its ability to dominate the market through regulation and contracting procedures; and
(3) the inability, at least in the past, of firms dependent on Defense Department contracts to manage successfully in the private sector.

Despite this domination, new opportunities have arisen in the civilian sector over the past fifteen years as a result of the enormous growth in commercial air traffic. These have paved the way toward less reliance on government support. Prime contractors, partic-ularly in the jet turbine market, have been especially successful in making the conversion.

How long this lasts will depend on the strength of the re-equipment cycle. When the cycle troughs out sometime in the mid to late 1980s, we may see an even more competitive domestic environment as firms scramble to secure additional government contracts to fill the void. What role increased defense spending will play in maintaining the boom beyond this period is uncertain.

Geographical Dispersion of Production

Ultimately, the fate of the workforce in the current production locations depends on the degree to which geographical dispersion of the industry occurs. The technological requirements for dispersion—falling transportation and communication costs—exist if the industry chooses to take further advantage of them. Whether it is profitable to do so depends in theory on:

(1) relative direct costs (labor, transportation, taxes, energy);
(2) the location of supplies of skilled labor;
(3) the demand for international co-production and joint venture agreements; and
(4) the extent of multiple sourcing and parallel production.

According to our analysis, we can generally dismiss relative costs as a major cause of the export of production from its traditional locations. This is particularly true of the New England segment of the industry where labor costs are relatively lower than in other areas, transportation costs are insignificant, and taxes and energy charges remain unimportant components of the overall cost structure of the industry.

The supply of skilled labor is probably a more important factor in determining the location of production facilities, but in the final analysis not a decisive one. As far as we can determine, no region boasts a large supply of readily employable machinists and machine operators, so the skilled-worker issue is problematic wherever industry chooses to locate.

The more important determinants of geographical dispersion, and indeed the ones that can explain, for example, the decline in the value added to value of shipments ratio in New England, are related to the production strategies listed in points 3 and 4 above. The changing nature of competition and the existence of international sources of capital are responsible for the increasing export of production and technology and, with this, the export of jobs. It is not clear whether individual firms have much control over these dynamics. Rather than suggest a "conspiracy" against U.S. communities and workers, it is probably more appropriate to blame the loss of domestic control of the industry on the nature of the competition itself. Increased rivalry for limited "big ticket" sales is a powerful incentive to seek out co-production partners, joint ventures, multiple sources, and parallel production facilities.

Recommendations from Industry and Union Representatives

During the course of this study, we queried industry sources about public policies that they would recommend to improve the future viability of the industry. Most of the policies they recommended involve action at the federal level.

1. Better long-term planning and more consistent government policy are needed. The erratic stop/go behavior of government procurement and funding policies is said to be harmful to the industry. In this regard, Harry Gray, Chairman of United Technologies Corporation, has remarked, "It takes a lot of people and a lot of resources to develop, manufacture, market, and service something as technologically complex as a jet engine. You can't turn planning and production on and off like a water faucet at the whim of some bureaucrat. You have to rely on well thought out, consistent governmental policies—policies that recognize the new realities."[2] The impermanence of the planning horizon makes it exceedingly difficult for firms to make investment decisions with any degree of certainty. A cohesive, long-range, national transportation policy, for example, would make it easier for firms to make long-term investment plans with greater confidence.

2. Prime contractors argue that if U.S. firms were allowed to more easily form joint ventures and combine capital resources, they would be less apt to seek foreign partners for development programs. This change would eliminate much of the employment and technology transfer that is currently taking place. In order to accomplish this, anti-trust laws must be relaxed.

3. To promote export sales, the Export-Import Bank should be strengthened by removing it from the unified budget, liberalizing its lending authority, and increasing the amount of funds it can make available in the form of loans.[3] Furthermore, some industry representatives would like to see domestic producers obtain the same favorable interest rate on borrowing that the Ex-Im Bank allows foreign airlines. Before delivering the airplane to the foreign purchaser, for example, the manufacturer would obtain the loan directly.

Upon delivery, the loan to the manufacturer could be terminated and assumed by the purchasing airline.[4]

4. Other recommendations for strengthening the industry's ability to enter international markets include the removal of tariff and non-tariff barriers that adversely affect export sales and the de-bureaucratization of export license administration. Industry leaders complain that export controls are used in an erratic and at times subjective and capricious manner. These controls, it is maintained, should be implemented only when national security is clearly threatened. In this regard, the industry argues that the federal government should separate foreign military sales from political and moral issues such as human rights. This issue alone, industry representatives claim, has blocked many potential orders that were subsequently filled by eager foreign firms.

5. Industry representatives also claim that technological superiority cannot be maintained if domestic firms are forced to continue their reliance on foreign sources for financial capital. To ensure the industry's long-run viability, the federal government must be willing to substantially increase funding for basic research and development. This support would promote technological superiority, or at least arrest the erosion of it.

6. As for federal taxation, the industry would benefit from higher investment tax credits and more liberal depreciation allowances on plant and equipment. Industry leaders argue that the rapid transformation of technology in the aircraft industry imposes faster depreciation than in other sectors of the economy.

7. Finally, in terms of meeting the skill shortage, industry leaders stress the need for a total rethinking and restructuring of the American educational system. Vocational education must be stressed at the expense of expanded liberal arts and sciences. As for on-the-job training, industry executives advocate direct training subsidization of apprenticeship programs by the government, a responsibility currently relegated to the industry itself.

In addition to probing industry representatives for public policy recommendations, we gathered suggestions for government and company policy from trade union sources. As noted in Chapter 6, the biggest threat facing aircraft unions is that posed by the growing internationalization of the industry, and therefore this area receives the most attention from union leaders.

1. Unions maintain that the federal government provides incentives through its tax laws for the export of jobs and technology. Specifically, tax deferrals and foreign tax credits are enjoyed by corporations that take their production abroad. Unions therefore urge the repeal of foreign tax deferrals and credits that encourage corporations to reduce their operations at home and expand abroad.
2. Internally, the leadership of unionized plants would like to gain greater control of subcontract activity. They suggest that this is possible by writing language into their contracts that would force firms to maintain employment in the union shop rather than utilize outside, normally non-union vendors.
3. Expansion of the Trade Readjustment Act (TRA) is one specific policy the unions would like to see implemented immediately. Union representatives advocate expanded severance pay and retraining benefits, simplified review procedures, and a more liberal interpretation of what is considered displacement as a result of international trade.
4. Expansion of government-supported training is another recommendation on which union officials urge immediate action. CETA should be expanded to include three- and four-year apprenticeship programs, and state vocational training programs should be reoriented toward high-skill, blue-collar occupations.
5. Finally, led by the national leadership of the IAM, some union officials advocate government inducements to coax defense firms to begin rational programs of peacetime conversion. Union officials maintain that if the industry does not place greater emphasis on conversion, their members will ultimately be shut out of the job market. One specific recommendation involves forcing defense firms to put aside a specific percentage of all defense department contract funds, which would be allocated for research and development on possible non-defense products.

These sets of recommendations are by no means all-inclusive, nor should they necessarily be construed as our own policy prescriptions. Their presentation simply highlights some of the policies that the industry views as necessary to maintain its competitive position in the international marketplace, and unions see as necessary to maintain employment and income security for their members.

Indeed, some of these recommendations might reduce the volatility of the industry or limit its trend toward geographical dispersion. There are real economic and political costs attached to each of them, however, and these costs must be weighed carefully against the potential benefits. What seems to be true is that the dynamics of the industry are determined by underlying systemic forces that are not amenable to quick or easy redirection. These forces call for a comprehensive and far-reaching policy if there is to be any significant change in the extremely volatile nature of the industry and its consequences for the workforce.

Planning for the Future

The coming decade will be a vital one for the American economy. With lagging productivity in a host of industrial sectors and increased foreign penetration in nearly all of them, the aircraft industry stands out as one of the few sectors that has maintained its international prestige and industrial might. Only the computer industry ranks with the aircraft industry in terms of the sophisticated technological products that the U.S. offers the world market. Unlike the automobile, steel, and rubber industries that now face rigorous competition from more productive and innovative firms in Europe and Japan, the domestic industry has no competition like that offered these other industries by Toyota, Datsun, Volkswagen, Nippon Steel, Michelin, and Bridgestone. Boeing, Pratt & Whitney, General Electric, McDonnell Douglas, and Lockheed still dominate the market, despite new arrivals like Airbus Industrie in Europe.

Nevertheless, in order to maintain the position of world leader in this specialized market, there seems to be a pressing need for better planning in both the public and private sectors. The cyclical volatility of the industry, unchecked by an explicit policy to smooth out both defense and commercial orders, threatens the economic viability of aircraft-dependent communities and, of course, the workers and subcontractors within them. The severity of the aircraft business cycle has tended to so disturb the planning horizon in the industry that fewer and fewer firms are left to compete in the market. Only those with immense cash reserves from past successes are able to mount the financial campaigns necessary to introduce new products. Already there is some evidence that McDonnell Douglas and Lockheed will sit out the current commercial re-equipment cycle, leaving the field entirely to Boeing and perhaps one or two European competitors. The result will be a near monopoly in this market segment.

It is perhaps with respect to labor that planning becomes most critical. The inability of firms to find adequate supplies of skilled aerospace engineers and machinists was the most significant constraint on the industry during the late 1970s. Too little attention was paid to this potential problem after Viet-Nam. Neither the government nor the private sector seems to have considered the need for training a new generation of skilled workers, although any cursory examination of demographic data on the post–World War II labor force would have easily indicated the nature of the problem. The federal government, as well as individual state governments, seemed to pay little attention to providing training in machine skills through federal and state training and apprenticeship programs, while the private sector—particularly during the industry recession—was unwilling to invest adequately in these essential skills. Smoothing out the aircraft cycle through better strategic planning would provide the industry with a better forecast of potential worker demand. This in turn would give more incentive to firms and workers to invest in training, knowing that this investment would not face premature depreciation.

Better planning is also needed for the inevitable "downtimes" in the industry. Seattle seemed almost totally unprepared for the economic calamity that accompanied the massive layoffs at Boeing and its local subcontractors in the early 1970s. Similarly, we know from research on the aircraft industry in Hartford County, Connecticut, that neither firms, workers, nor community organizations were prepared for the widespread layoffs and forced early retirements that accompanied the cutback in aircraft orders for Pratt & Whitney and Hamilton-Standard in the years after 1968.[5] Subcontractors went out of business by the dozen while literally thousands of workers and their families had to find ways to get by without jobs they had come to depend on. The community, as well as local employers, was totally unprepared for the number of unemployed created by the convergence of sales declines in both the defense and commercial sectors. Some form of "preparedness planning," which has become commonplace in areas where natural disasters are apt to occur, should be implemented in local areas where aircraft production dominates.

There also appears to be a need to focus on the special problems of the aircraft industry subcontractor. Given the exceptionally high business and financial risk in the industry, conventional financial institutions have been wary of providing venture capital to this segment of the market. As a result, many small but otherwise viable subcontractors are forced out of business and many others never even have the chance to start up. For many the final option is either to become a target for acquisition by another firm or to cease operations entirely. If the subcontractor market is to remain profitable in the U.S., it may be necessary to consider government-aided financing or risk sharing. Naturally this is a highly charged political question that must be addressed from both a normative and an objective perspective.

Finally, a real question is arising about the nature of the industry, which is becoming more concentrated and potentially less competitive as many firms exit from the market. It may be necessary to consider ways of making it easier for domestic producers to form joint ventures, as industry leaders have proposed. In this case, however, the industry must be considered more like a natural monopoly similar to a public utility. This may require as a *quid pro quo* for reduced anti-trust activity a greater degree of government regulation to ensure that the industry operates in the public interest. Again, this is a political issue that demands thoughtful debate.

What can be said definitively is that the aircraft industry provides us with an example of what is both the best and the worst in the American economy. It is an industry that has captured our imaginations from the earliest days of this century and provided us with an opportunity for displaying our finest technological ingenuity. Communities have been created around this industry and millions of workers have found well-paying jobs building the aircraft that defend the country and fly us where we must go on business and where we wish to go for pleasure.

Yet there is another side of the industry that must not be overlooked. Because of its extraordinary volatility, the industry is fraught with economic insecurity. Neither firms nor workers and their communities have ever been able to count on the industry to provide long-term secure incomes. From now through perhaps the better part of this decade, the industry will provide a veritable feast for the firms connected to it. Many workers will benefit as well, although the geographic dispersion of production will no doubt reduce the employment opportunities that might otherwise have been created. Whether famine follows the current feast, as has been the tradition in the industry, depends on whether the private sector, working with an enlightened government, can find the secret to smoothing out the aerospace business cycle and thereby, for the first time, provide a secure planning horizon for all those dependent upon this sector. This is the real challenge of the 1980s.

Endnotes

1. Aerospace Industries Association, *Aerospace Facts and Figures 1980/81,* August 1980, p. 11.
2. "Foreign Economic Policies Criticized," *Aviation Week,* May 7, 1979, p. 69.
3. "The Leadership Forum," *Aerospace Magazine,* January 1971, p. 12.
4. *Ibid.*
5. Paula Rayman and Barry Bluestone, *The Private and Social Costs of Job Loss in the Aircraft Industry: A Metrostudy,* Social Welfare Research Institute, Boston College, 1981 (forthcoming).

Appendix

PRODUCTS OF THE AIRCRAFT AND PARTS INDUSTRY (SIC 372)

SIC 3721 Aircraft
Aircraft
Airplanes, fixed or rotary wings
Airships
Balloons (aircraft)
Dirigibles
Gliders (aircraft)
Helicopters

SIC 3724 Aircraft engines and engine parts
Air scoops, aircraft
Aircraft engine starting vibrators
Aircraft engines and engine parts, internal combustion and jet propulsion
Cooling systems, aircraft engine
Engine heaters, aircraft
Engine mount parts, aircraft
Exhaust systems, aircraft
External power units, for hand inertia starters, aircraft
Jet-assisted takeoff devices (JATO)
Lubricating systems, aircraft
Pumps, aircraft engine
Rocket motors, aircraft
Starters, aircraft: nonelectric
Turbines, aircraft type
Turbo-superchargers, aircraft

189

SIC 3728 **Aircraft parts and auxiliary equipment, not elsewhere classified**

Accumulators, aircraft propeller
Actuators, aircraft: mechanical, electrical, and hydraulic
Adapter assemblies, hydromatic propeller
Ailerons, aircraft
Aircraft armament, except guns
Aircraft arresting device system
Aircraft assemblies, subassemblies, and parts, except engines
Aircraft body assemblies and parts
Aircraft power transmission equipment
Aircraft propeller parts
Airframe assemblies, except for guided missiles
Airplane brake expanders
Alighting assemblies (landing gear), aircraft
Beaching gear, aircraft
Blades, aircraft propeller: metal or wood
Bomb racks, aircraft
Brakes, aircraft
Chaffing dispensers, aircraft
Controls: hydraulic and pneumatic, aircraft
Countermeasure dispensers, aircraft
De-icing equipment, aircraft
Dive brakes, aircraft
Dusting and spraying equipment, aircraft
Dynetric balancing stands, aircraft
Elevators, aircraft
Empennage (tail) assemblies and parts, aircraft
Fins, aircraft
Flaps, aircraft wing
Fluid power and control components, aircraft
Fuel tanks, aircraft: including self-sealing
Fuselage assemblies, aircraft
Gears, power transmission, aircraft
Governors, aircraft propeller feathering
Hubs, aircraft propeller
Hydraulic pumps, valves, and cylinders, aircraft
Instrument panel mockups, aircraft training units
Landing gear, aircraft

SIC 3728   *(cont.)*

Landing skis and tracks, aircraft
Link trainers (aircraft training mechanisms)
Nacelles, aircraft
Oleo struts, aircraft
Oxygen systems, for aircraft
Panel assemblies (hydromatic propeller test stands), aircraft
Pontoons, aircraft
Power transmission equipment, aircraft
Propeller alining tables
Propellers, variable and fixed pitch: and parts, aircraft
Pumps, propeller feathering
Refueling equipment, airplane: for use in flight
Roto-blades for helicopters
Rudders, aircraft
Seat ejector devices, aircraft
Spinners, aircraft propeller
Stabilizers, aircraft
Tanks, fuel: aircraft
Target drones
Targets, trailer type: aircraft
Tow targets
Training aids, aircraft: except electronic
Transmissions, aircraft
Turret test fixtures, aircraft
Turrets and turret drives, aircraft
Wheels, aircraft
Wing assemblies and parts, aircraft

BIBLIOGRAPHY

Aerospace Industries Association. *Aerospace Facts and Figures 1978/79*. New York: McGraw-Hill, 1978.

———. *Aerospace Facts and Figures 1980/81*. New York: McGraw Hill, 1980.

Aerospace Magazine. "The Leadership Forum." January 1971, p. 12.

American Metal Market. "GE Board Approves $3 Million Aircraft Engine Plant Expansion." July 2, 1979, p. 17.

———. "GE's Engine Group Will Set Up Airfoils Forge, Cast Plant in Ky." December 3, 1979, p. 20.

———. "McDonnell Douglas Expands DNC Machining." March 12, 1979, p. 12.

———. "P&WA Adding to Test Facilities." September 11, 1978, p. 41.

———. "Sikorsky Set to Construct Copter Plant." April 3, 1978, p. 18.

———. "Sikorsky to Establish Separate R&D Center with Personnel Shifts." August 14, 1978, p. 11.

Arthur D. Little, Inc. *Fostering Industrial Growth in Massachusetts Vol. I: Cutbacks in Defense Spending and the Economy of Massachusetts, 1968–1972*. Report prepared for the Department of Commerce and Development, Commonwealth of Massachusetts, October 1970, p. 62.

Avco Corporation. *Annual Report 1978*. Wilmington, Massachusetts.

Aviation Week and Space Technology. "Air France Postpones Decision on Powerplant for Airbus A310's." October 8, 1979, p. 30.

———. "Foreign Economic Policies Criticized." May 7, 1979, p. 67.

———. "French Airline Selects CF6 for Its A310's." December 31, 1979, p. 16.

———. "General Electric Engines Ordered for A310." August 25, 1980, p. 26.

———. "GE President Sees Continuing Gains in Jet Engine Business." December 27, 1965, p. 29.

———. "U.S. Pressed to Meet Helicopter Demand." June 2, 1969, p. 343.

———. "Washington Roundup." October 10, 1966, p. 25.

BALL, ROBERT. "Who's That Chasing After Boeing," *Fortune*. April 21, 1980, p. 138.

BANKS, ROD. "The Big Commercial Engines," *Interavia*. June 1977, p. 541.

BARANSON, JACK. "Technology Transfer: Effects on U.S. Competitiveness and Employment," *The Impact of International Trade and Investment on Employment*. Washington, D.C.: Bureau of International Affairs, U.S. Department of Labor, 1978.

BECKER, GARY S. *Human Capital*. New York: NBER, 1964.

BLAIR, JOHN. *Economic Concentration*. New York: Harcourt Brace Jovanovich, 1972.

Boston Globe. "Considering Size, New England Tops in Defense Work." July 18, 1979.

————. "Pratt and Whitney Gets $450M Pact From American." December 23, 1980, p. 36.

————. "52.8b OK'd for Defense." August 27, 1980, p. 3.

BOULTON, DAVID. "F-16: Arms Sale of the Century." Boston, Mass.: WGBH Educational Foundation, 1979. Script from WGBH television series "World," appearing March 15, 1979.

BRIGHT, CHARLES D. *The Jet Makers*. Lawrence, Kansas: Regents Press, 1979.

BULBAN, ERWIN J. "Backlogs Spurring Helicopter Industry," *Aviation Week and Space Technology*. March 13, 1978, p. 200.

————. "General Aviation Sees Equipment Boom," *Aviation Week and Space Technology*. December 12, 1975, p. 12.

————. "Helicopter Market Growth Continues," *Aviation Week and Space Technology*. March 3, 1980, p. 219.

Business Week. "A Costly Package for Aerospace Peace." August 3, 1968, p. 78.

————. "Military Cutbacks Send Tremors Through Industry." December 6, 1969, p. 23.

————. "Military Helicopters Get Chopped Down." August 29, 1970, p. 58.

————. "Pratt and Whitney Feels the Pangs of Success." August 6, 1966.

————. "The Rivalry Intensifies for Airbus Engines." November 5, 1979, p. 68.

CARLEY, WILLIAM. "Boeing Reign in Skies May Last a Long Time as Competition Fades," *Wall Street Journal*. December 19, 1980, p. 1.

————. "United Technologies Plans New Engine for Jet Airplanes in a $1 Billion Project," *Wall Street Journal*. November 30, 1979, p. 14.

CHAKRAVARTY, SUBRATA. "What Price Pride," *Forbes*. July 7, 1980, p. 38.

CORDINER, RALPH. *New Frontiers for Professional Managers*. New York: McGraw Hill, 1956.

ESTALL, R. C. *New England: A Study in Industrial Adjustment*. New York: Praeger Publishers, 1966.

Financial Post. "Pratt and Whitney Pins Hopes on Lightweight Engines." November 3, 1962, p. 62.

Financial Times. "Aerospatiale May Build Helicopters in America." March 1, 1978, p. 5.

Forbes. "Aerospace and Defense." January 1, 1969, p. 138.

————. "Can the Pentagon Mix Maseratis and VW's?" January 15, 1973, p. 19.

————. February 1, 1973, p. 34.

————. "Rocky Ride on Route 128," September 1, 1965, p. 32.

Fortune. "McDonnell Douglas Is Flying Scared." August 25, 1980, p. 42.

General Electric Company. *Securities and Exchange Commission Form 10K.* For the fiscal year ended December 31, 1978.

George D. Hall Company. *Directory of New England Manufacturers:* Boston: Alpine Press, 1978.

GIDDES, J. PHILLIP. "Giants Battle in U.S. Small Turbine Market," *Interavia.* March 18, 1977, p. 179.

GOLD, HAROLD. "Aerospace Exports Face Key Legislation." *Journal of Commerce.* January 1, 1969, p. 23.

GOLDSAND, ALAN. *Journal of Commerce.* November 13, 1972, p. 3.

GORDON, ROBERT J. "$45 Billion of U.S. Private Investment Has Been Mislaid," *American Economic Review.* June 1969.

GRIFFITHS, DAVID. "Air Force Studies Impact of Engine Delivery Delay," *Aviation Week and Space Technology.* October 8, 1979, p. 22.

HALLORAN, RICHARD. "Why Defense Costs so Much," *New York Times.* January 11, 1981, p. F1.

Hartford Courant. "P&WA Said Lured by Cheap Maine Labor." December 28, 1978, p. 3.

Hartford Times. "Pratt and Whitney 50th Anniversary." October 3, 1975, p. 7.

HILL, CHRISTIAN G. "Lockheed Posts 2nd Quarter Loss of $26.6 Million," *Wall Street Journal.* July 30, 1980, p. 5.

HOTZ, ROBERT. "Business Flying Boom Continues," *Aviation Week and Space Technology.* September 26, 1977, p. 13.

————. "Outlook for 1971," *Aviation Week and Space Technology.* January 11, 1971, p. 9.

IAM. *Shoptalk.* February 14, 1977.

————. *Shoptalk.* February 28, 1977.

IAM Research Department. *1980 IAM Aerospace Report: Economic Outlook.* International Association of Machinists, April 1980.

Industry Week. "A Big Contract for Sikorsky." January 17, 1971, p. 15.

————. "Sweeteners for Foreign Aircraft Sales." May 28, 1979, p. 86.

————. "Why Appalachia?" December 13, 1971, p. 47.

Iron Age. "Industrial Briefs." October 11, 1976, p. 23.

————. "Aerospace Sales Boom Breaks Success Barrier." July 25, 1968, p. 92.

————. "Pratt and Whitney Spends Lavishly to Avoid Machining." August 29, 1977, p. 78.

JOHNSEN, KATHERINE. "DOD Civil Export Control Rule Urged," *Aviation Week and Space Technology*. March 19, 1979, p. 27.

————. "Views Divided on Export Growth Rate," *Aviation Week and Space Technology*. July 3, 1978, p. 68.

Journal of Commerce. "Sikorsky Contracted for Chopper." December 24, 1976, p. 2.

Kaman Corporation. *1977 Annual Report*.

KIRBY, CHARLES. "Computer Aided Design/Production Equipment." Thesis for M.B.A. degree, Boston College, 1970.

KOLCUM, EDWARD. "Foreign Gains Threaten U.S. Lead," *Aviation Week and Space Technology*. November 27, 1978, p. 14.

LARSEN, RAY. "Copter Pact Spurs $100 Million Sikorsky Expansion," *American Metal Market*. March 6, 1978, p. 5.

————. "$1 Billion in Subpacts Seen Offshoot of Sikorsky Army Helicopter Awards," *American Metal Market*. January 10, 1977, p. 1.

————. "Sikorsky Will Take Helicopter Transmission Output In-House," *American Metal Market*. March 7, 1977, p. 1.

LENOROVITZ, JEFFREY. "United CFM56 Selection Sparks DC-8 Retrofit," *Aviation Week and Space Technology*. April 9, 1979, p. 18.

LONDON, MICHAEL. "P&WA Buys Maine Plant," *Hartford Courant*. December 26, 1978, p. 1.

LONGCOPE, KAY. "Big Industry in Small Town Has Fans, Detractors," *Boston Globe*. January 21, 1979, p. 21.

MELMAN, SEYMOUR. *The Defense Economy: Conversion of Industries and Occupations to Civilian Needs*. New York: Praeger Publishers, 1970.

MILLER, JOHN A. *Men and Volts at War*. New York: McGraw Hill, 1947.

Moody's Investor Services. *Moody's Industrial Manual*. New York, 1978.

New England Business. "Sikorsky Quits U.S. Coast Guard Bidding." April 16, 1979, p. 7.

New England Congressional Caucus. *DOD Prime Contract Awards: A Regional Analysis, 1951–1978*. July 1979.

New England Regional Commission. *Occupational Training Information in New England*, Volume II. September 1978, p. 79.

New York Times. "U.S. Lifts Ban on Jet Engine Venture with France's SNECMA." June 23, 1973, p. 37.

————. "Will the Industry Sink into Obscurity after Vietnam?" August 20, 1975, p. F1.

Office of Community Development and Planning, City of Hartford. *Comprehensive Development Strategies*. May 1979.

Office of Management and Budget. *Standard Industrial Classification Manual 1972*. Washington, D.C.: U.S. Government Printing Office, 1972.

O'LONE, RICHARD. "Engineer Lack Worries Boeing," *Aviation Week and Space Technology*. February 12, 1979, p. 12.

———. "Pace of 757 Orders Raising Concern," *Aviation Week and Space Technology*. July 21, 1980, p. 43.

OTT, JAMES. "Industry Leaders Rap U.S. Export Policy," *Aviation Week and Space Technology*. May 7, 1979, p. 19.

PECK, MERTON, AND FREDERICK SCHERER. *The Weapons Acquisition Process: An Economic Analysis*. Cambridge, Mass.: Harvard University, 1962.

PHILLIPS, AMARIN. *Technology and Market Structure: A Study of the Aircraft Industry*. Lexington, Mass.: D.C. Heath, 1971.

PILLSBURY, FRED. "Air Deregulation: Bonanza and a Bust," *Boston Globe*. April 6, 1979.

QUALTROUGH, SUSAN, AND JOSEPH JABLONOWSKI. "Filling the Need for Skilled Workers," *American Machinist*. June 1979.

RAE, JOHN B. *Climb to Greatness: The American Aircraft Industry 1920–1960*. Cambridge, Mass.: MIT Press, 1968.

RUDNITSKY, HOWARD, AND GERALD ODENING. "Jet Wars," *Forbes*. August 18, 1980, p. 35.

SIEKMAN, PHILLIP. "The Big New Whirl in Helicopters," *Fortune*. April 1966, p. 124.

SIMONSON, G. R., ed. *The History of the American Aircraft Industry*. Cambridge, Mass.: MIT Press, 1968.

SMITH, ANSON. "The GE Touch: Massachusetts Getting More Military Contracts Thanks to the Company's Winning Ways," *Boston Globe*. December 10, 1978, p. D8.

Standard and Poor's Corporation. "Basic Aerospace Analysis," *Industry Surveys*. New York: McGraw Hill, December 1978.

———. "Basic Air Transport Analysis," *Industry Surveys*. New York: McGraw Hill, April, 1978.

———. "The Outlook: Demand for Commercial Jets to Stir Sales." December 1978.

State and National Apprenticeship System (SNAPS). *Apprentice Registration Actions by Personal Characteristics within Selected Occupational Groups*. State Summary, 1976.

Steel. "Aerospace Firms Leaning Heavily on Overtime." July 10, 1967.

———. "Aerospace Giants Still Suffering Growing Pains." March 27, 1967, p. 150.

Time. "Masters of the Air." April 7, 1980, p. 54.

———. "No Market for the Jumbos." February 2, 1976, p. 50.

TRAINER, GLYNNIS. *The Metalworking Machinery Industry*. Joint Center for Urban Studies, Harvard-MIT, 1979.

United Technologies Corporation. *First Quarter Report*. April 10, 1979.

———. *1977 Annual Report*.

U.S. Bureau of the Census. *Annual Survey of Manufacturers*. Washington, D.C.: U.S. Government Printing Office, 1960–1976.

————. *County Business Patterns*. Washington, D.C.: U.S. Government Printing Office, 1959–1976.

U.S. Congress, House Subcommittee on Special Investigations of Small Business Problems of the Select Committee on Small Business, *Problems of the Tool and Die Industry and Associated Problems of Manufacturers and Distributors of Machine Tools: Hearings on H. Res. 13*, 89th Congress, 2nd Session, July 26–27, 1966, p. 85.

U.S. Department of Defense. *Annual Report Fiscal Year 1979*. Washington, D.C.: U.S. Government Printing Office, February 2, 1978.

————. *Departmental Industrial Plant Reserve Report*. September 1978.

U.S. Department of Health, Education and Welfare. *Vocational and Technical Education Annuals*. Fiscal Years 1963–1976.

U.S. Department of Labor, Bureau of Labor Statistics. *Analysis of Work Stoppages*. Annual surveys 1960–1976.

U.S. Department of Labor, Bureau of Labor Statistics, Division of Wages and Industrial Relations. *Work Stoppages: Aircraft and Parts Industry, 1927–1959*. January 1961.

U.S. Department of Labor, Bureau of Labor Statistics. *Employment and Earnings Statistics for the United States 1909–1968*. Bulletin No. 1312-6. Washington, D.C.: U.S. Government Printing Office, August 1968.

————. *Employment and Earnings*. Washington, D.C.: U.S. Government Printing Office, monthly reports 1978–1980.

WALD, MATTHEW. "The New Breed of Helicopters," *New York Times*. February 12, 1979, p. D1.

Wall Street Journal. "Pratt & Whitney's Output Lags; Strikes at Suppliers Cited." September 17, 1979, p. 4.

————. "Pratt and Whitney Plans to Spend $103 Million to Increase Capacity." December 5, 1979, p. 45.

————. "Unit of Boeing to Pay $44.8 Million to GSA for Plant in Wichita." December 7, 1979, p. 5.

WEBER, ALFRED. *Theory of the Location of Industries*. Chicago: University of Chicago Press, 1929.

WELLES, NANCY. "The 50 Leading Exporters," *Fortune*. September 22, 1980, p. 115.

WETMORE, WARREN. "Supplier Strikes Worry Engine Maker," *Aviation Week and Space Technology*. July 23, 1979, p. 23.

WILLIAMS, WINSTON. "Engine Maker Works on Image," *New York Times*. December 26, 1979, p. D2.

WINTHROP, GRANT. "A Rival Finally Comes Up to Speed," *Fortune*. December 17, 1979, p. 64.

YAEGER, DON. "McDonnell Douglas Doubles DNC Use," *American Metal Market*. December 12, 1977, p. 12.

YAFFE, MICHAEL. "War, Changes Strain Aerospace Industry," *Aviation Week and Space Technology*. December 14, 1966, p. 65.

INDEX